THE CAMBRIDGE PHENOMENON

THE CAMBRIDGE PHENOMENON

The Growth of High Technology Industry in a University Town

Segal Quince & Partners

First published 1985 by
Segal Quince & Partners
Hall Keeper's House
42 Castle Street
Cambridge
CB3 0AJ
England

Published in association with
Brand Brothers and Co, London E9

Design and production in association with
Book Production Consultants, Cambridge
Text design and map artwork by
Carrods Graphic Design, Cambridge
Cover design and family tree artwork by
Portfolio Design Consultants, Swavesey, Cambridge
Typeset by Cambridge Photosetting Services,
Cambridge
Printed in Great Britain by The Thetford Press,
Thetford, Norfolk

TABLE OF CONTENTS

FOREWORD BY THE VICE CHANCELLOR OF THE UNIVERSITY OF CAMBRIDGE

It is a pleasure to introduce this report which is a fascinating case study of the role of scientific research and development in economic growth and change. The report complements in a most interesting way the debate in Britain of a decade of more ago over the right balance between basic and applied research and development, and also the then favoured principle of customer-orientation in research commissioned by government.

What makes this report so important is that – at a time when long-term research is under increasingly severe financial pressure – it is an empirical study of the processes of research-based invention and innovation and their commercial exploitation. It brings into the open the direct and indirect role that a university (in this case Cambridge) can play in fostering these processes. And it highlights the benefits of a university's being cognisant of the prime importance in all this of academics being encouraged to think – after all, universities ought to be good at thinking, it is their main stock in trade – and to create new opportunities for their individual expression.

My moral tutor Nevill Coghill – Oxford's first professor of drama, a mediaeval scholar and quintessentially an arts man – once remarked to me that the number of creative minds in any generation was limited and that many who in early days would have found careers in the arts today achieved success in the sciences. Coghill greatly admired Heisenberg and was particularly impressed by the sheer imaginative thinking involved in wave mechanics.

If this view of creative scientific thinking is correct it is clear that the thinkers will require plenty of encouragement and careful handling but probably as little direct management as possible. Universities should provide them with the facilities to help their ideas flourish, and then stand back as far as possible and avoid intervening or distracting them with tidy administrative procedures.

Coghill's remarks were made long ago and in another place but I am delighted, all these years later, to find myself in the succession of Vice Chancellors who have had – as the present report brings out so clearly – a proper respect for the individual's scientific talents and creativity and his freedom to exploit them. This policy has had to be balanced, carefully and quietly, at the University or administrative level to guard against any abuse of responsibilities at the laboratory or faculty level and against other dangers. In pursuing this approach, we believe so far successfully, we have indeed been well served by our principal administrative officers.

Clearly Cambridge's growing prominence as a centre of science-based industry stems directly and indirectly from many factors, not just the University's policy of leaving creative individuals as free as possible.

Much must be attributed to the general atmosphere of scientific excellence that has been generated for well over 100 years. The presence of the vigorous college system alongside the University has been important in many respects – not least through the attraction of college life helping make it possible for the University and local research institutions to recruit scientists of the highest quality. Nor should one neglect more subtle influences: for instance, the way in which conversation between the fellows in the colleges can spark off fruitful ideas (such as obviously passed between Coghill, the mediaeval scholar, and Hinshelwood, the physical chemist, both at Exeter College, Oxford).

These influences are explored and assessed in this book, and also put into a proper perspective relative to the many other factors that have shaped Cambridge's success in advanced technological industry. These factors include, for instance, the relative isolation of the place (though that is now changing), its sequestration from industrial society as it has evolved in Britain's cities since the last century, and the active role played by the local financial and business community and by the local authorities.

There has indeed been an extraordinary concatenation of events since the Stourbridge Fair of the twelfth century or so, which probably left a lot of accommodation available and so made Cambridge a place where the men from Merton realised students could stay from harvest until sowing time (the so-called academical year). And the events are far from played out yet.

There is a local excitement of it all. The visiting financier or industrialist, so often now from overseas, soon discovers this when the taxi driver from the railway station is full of information (gossip even) about the University; like the story about Lord Butler's now legendary remark at high table in Trinity to the foreign ambassador who was waxing eloquent about his country's educational system – "You do realise, your Excellency, that this small college has borne more Nobel prizewinners than your whole country, don't you?" (Indeed read on and you will find this anecdote referred to in the report.)

The question must be asked: what does the University get out of the liberal policies referred to earlier? Will those who get rich put anything back? And if they do, won't it be to their colleges rather than to the University which they so often see just as an examinations body? Indeed it has to be acknowledged how often graduates have made gifts to their colleges in the past.

But the University too has had its great gifts. The annual service for the commemoration of benefactors in Great St Mary's refers not only to the "acts of personal munificence which we have received at the hands of our Sovereigns" but also records that "In 1816 Richard Viscount Fitzwilliam of Trinity Hall bequeathed his magnificent collection of pictures, engravings and books, together with £100 000 – and by this princely bequest enabled us to build the Fitzwilliam Museum".

Similar benefactions happily continue. For example, Herchel Smith, the chemist who started at Oxford and later worked in Lord Todd's department here going on to patent the alternative contraceptive pill, has recently founded and supported two chairs in our medical school.

So whatever may have been all the other factors underlying scientific and industrial success here in Cambridge, the policy of freedom of action and conscience for the individual researcher seems to be working and yielding tangible benefits to the University, and to the wider community too.

Of course it requires constant vigilance to ensure that interaction with commerce or industry does not distort our academic standards or distract us from the need to think hard. But there are benefits here too – who could deny that a good dose of contact with the outside business world does not help ensure that our teaching, thinking and research are on sensible lines in relevant subjects?

There are doubtless many lessons to be derived from this fascinating account of what has come to be called the Cambridge phenomenon. Two stand out in my mind: the fundamental importance of freedom for the individual, and the challenge to a university to play a full role in achieving economic growth and creating jobs while conserving vigorously its own cultural traditions and academic standards.

John Butterfield
1984

1
INTRODUCTION

BACKGROUND TO THE STUDY

1.1 This is a study of the so-called 'Cambridge phenomenon': the growing numbers of advanced technology companies established in and around the university and market town of Cambridge, England. It has been known for at least the past five years in some banking quarters and in the area itself that something interesting was happening in Cambridge by way of the start-up and growth of indigenous high technology companies linked in some way to the University. Despite a number of articles in the national press in 1981 and the probable analogies with the well-known growth of high technology industry around Boston (12) and Palo Alto (29), it has however been only in the past year or so that there has been wider recognition of the fact of a phenomenon and consequently outside interest in it.

1.2 It is no accident that the heightened interest has arisen only quite recently. For what is going on in Cambridge is directly relevant to four interrelated topics that have emerged in the past couple of years as having special significance to economic performance and policy at national and local levels. The issues are at present most strongly evident in Britain but there is no doubt of their growing importance in other European countries.

1.3 The first topic concerns the role of small new technology based firms (NTBFs) in the economy. They are attracting particular attention because, based chiefly on US experience, they are thought to have greater growth potential than conventional firms as well as to be better 'converters' of science into marketable products than large firms. Being small and young they are also held to be more flexible and opportunistic in responding to change than most well established businesses. At the same time there is a concern that they tend to over-emphasise the purely technological side of their businesses and neglect the marketing and financial aspects, and consequently will suffer an undue proportion of failures. More systematic knowledge is needed of NTBFs to inform public debate and policy.

1.4 Second, there is the question of links between industry and higher educational and research institutions. The latter bodies are increasingly looked at as possessing substantial resources of know-how and specialist physical facilities that are not being effectively harnessed, either to meet the technological develop-

ment needs of industry no matter where it is located or to contribute specifically to stimulating the local economies of the areas where they are based. Some would argue that the academic and research institutions themselves now also have a powerful financial motivation to increase their business contacts with the outside world, as most of them come under financial pressure arising from public expenditure restraints. The question is: under what circumstances, spontaneous or designed, do academic-industry links flourish?

1.5 A particular feature of the academic-industry scene in Britain at present is the large number of universities (and polytechnics) getting involved in science parks or at least planning or contemplating doing so. The concept of a science park – as providing not just industrial space easily accessible to a university but especially a focal point for university-industry interaction – is simple. But how well do science parks (or innovation or technology centres as they are variously called) work in practice in facilitating such synergy and technology transfer, and are the substantial monies being invested in them around the country being applied in the most effective way to realise these wider benefits?

1.6 The third issue is that of the particular contributions and relative roles of the public and private sectors in stimulating technological change and economic development. What is the long-term impact of the allocation of public research funds? How effective are the numerous government schemes for promoting innovation? How do local planning policies impinge on the high technology sector? What influence is being exercised by the financial and property development sectors? These are some of the questions that arise.

1.7 Fourth, the scale and pace of recent industrial change in Britain is increasingly seen as having associated with it an uneven regional impact. In general and highly simplified terms, the long established industrial and urban areas are experiencing further decline while market towns and rural areas, notably in attractive and reasonably accessible parts of the country, are experiencing growth of new industry. High technology companies are thought to be a significant element in this latter growth. Based on the Cambridge experience, what can be said about the evolving spatial distribution of high technology industry, and of economic activity more generally, in the country as a whole?

1.8 These four issues provide the overall framework and rationale of this study. But there is a further, more particular factor too. The fact that it is about Cambridge and not just any market town or university gives the subject a wider appeal. A story about one of the world's oldest and most famous universities becoming a vital element in development of a flourishing community of high technology small firms is clearly of interest in its own right.

1.9 The foregoing sets the general context of the study. The particular factors that brought the study about are these. In June 1983 a report, by the Advisory Council for Applied Research and Development and the Advisory Board of Research Councils, into links between higher educational institutions and industry was published (2). This drew attention, in passing, to the Cambridge phenomenon and observed that it would be instructive if it were better understood and any general lessons for university-industry links disseminated. Over the next seven months discussions took place between a variety of parties, reflecting both national and local as well as public and private sector interests, and eventually in February 1984 the present study was launched. Details of the sponsorship and organisation of the study are given in appendix A.

PURPOSE OF THE STUDY
1.10 The study had two broad objectives:
(a) to describe, quantify and analyse the Cambridge phenomenon, to identify the principal factors that have caused and shaped it, and to comment on its future prospects;
(b) to use the Cambridge experience to illuminate the four policy issues discussed.

1.11 The report is written with these two purposes in mind. In the second category in particular, we have drawn on wider experience of all the topics concerned and not just on this Cambridge study to seek to reach conclusions.

APPROACH TO THE STUDY
1.12 This has been a large exercise, covering a wide territory and both raising and confronting many issues of detail and technical complexity. Nevertheless, our concern throughout has been to 'tell a story' and to explain it, and to do so in a manner that is accessible and useful to a wide and diverse audience. Consequently discussion of methodology and presentation of de-

tailed statistical material are kept to a minimum. The interested reader is referred to appendix C for a brief statement of the approach and scope of the study.

1.13 Much of what the study deals with is made up of very recent history and current events, in which the principal actors are fairly easily identifiable. We were also given a great deal of information in confidence. Consequently the report has had to strike a balance between being a descriptive and analytical piece that refrained from 'naming names', and being something that would be rather livelier in style but run the risk of infringing the confidences and sensitivities that inevitably arise. Because a purpose of the study is to produce a report of interest and relevance outside Cambridge, we have tended towards the first kind of report, and we have sought to enliven it by inclusion of profiles of 'typical' Cambridge companies (including those six companies who were among our sponsors) and of some of the other organisations, developments and decisions that have been of significance on the Cambridge scene.

ORGANISATION OF THE REPORT
1.14 With this general approach in mind, the report is organised as follows. Following this introduction, the next chapter sets the scene of recent developments in Cambridge by presenting an historical perspective of industrial development in the area and on the changes leading up to the current phenomenon. Chapters 3 and 4 contain the primary empirical material generated by the study, viz information about the population of high technology companies in the area. This is followed in chapter 5 by discussion of the principal factors causing and shaping the phenomenon, based on the many general consultations we held in the course of the fieldwork.

1.15 Chapter 6 discusses the business development problems encountered by the young high technology firms as they grow. Chapter 7 represents a mild digression from the main thrust of the report in that it draws on the specific Cambridge experience and on knowledge gained elsewhere, to discuss issues of fundamental importance to the future of university-industry links in Britain. Finally, chapter 8 explores the prospects and issues for the phenomenon in the future; and a postscript discusses possible development in Cambridge of a teaching and research capability in business/management studies oriented specifically to the needs of small high technology companies.

1.16 Methodological and other topics not central to the main text are included in appendices at the end of the report. A genealogy of the companies is presented in a pull-out chart in chapter 3.

ACKNOWLEDGMENTS
1.17 We are indebted in many ways to many different organisations and individuals. Our principal acknowledgments are given in appendix B, and we would only wish to say here that without the enthusiastic cooperation of hundreds of people, including our sponsors and of course the companies themselves, this study would never have been completed.

2

INDUSTRIAL DEVELOPMENT IN THE CAMBRIDGE AREA – AN HISTORICAL PERSPECTIVE

INTRODUCTION

2.1 The purpose of this chapter is to put the recent and current business developments in Cambridge into a wider context of past sub-regional and regional economic development. For while these developments in Cambridge are the result principally of numerous Cambridge-specific factors (as will be seen later), they have also been materially influenced by physical infra-structure and other changes happening in the wider area, not least the city's location in one of the UK's fastest growing and economically resilient regions. Also, the current phenomenon must be seen against a backcloth of long-standing and special links between the University and local industry.

REGIONAL CONTEXT*

2.2 Cambridgeshire, of which Cambridge located in the south of the county is the principal city, forms the western part of the region of East Anglia (see map 2.1). Until some 25 years ago this region was long regarded as something of a rural backwater, albeit with fine historic towns such as Cambridge and Norwich and a prosperous agricultural sector, as well as a few towns such as Peterborough and Huntingdon with a successful record of manufacturing industry. The population was small and dispersed and the general sense of remote-ness and slow change was underlined by the poor transport links with the rest of the country.

2.3 Around 1960, however, change started taking place rapidly, principally as a result of people and industry previously based in London and the South East relocating to the region. Movement from these congested areas had of course been happening already, partly facilitated by the new and expanded towns programmes of the early post-war period. But initially the concentration of growth was mostly in towns closest to London and the South East, and it was not until the 1960s that the scale of change in East Anglia became appreciable.

2.4 In 1981 the population of the region was a little over 1.8 million, an increase of about 28% over the previous two decades. This growth was the largest among all regions but East Anglia still accounted in 1981 for only just over 3% of the UK total and it had by far the lowest population density of all the English regions. The chief component of population change

*This section draws in part on several published studies (15, 19, 21).

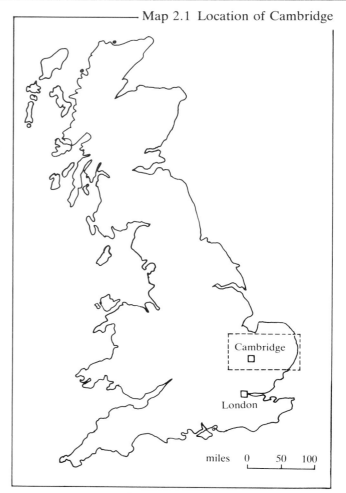

Map 2.1 Location of Cambridge

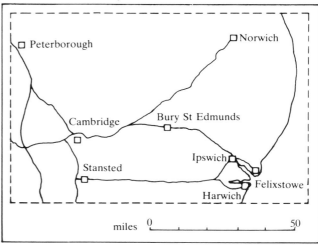

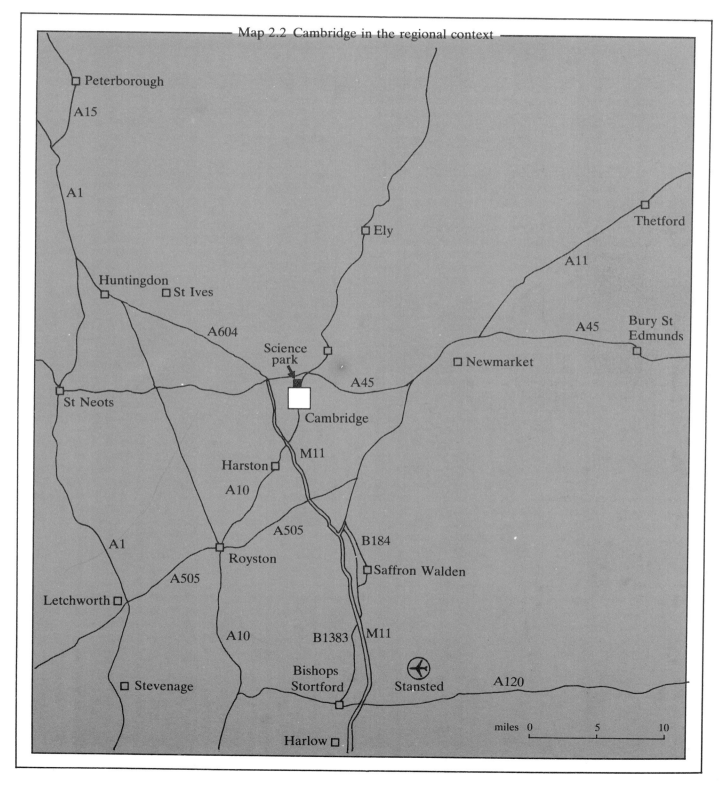

Map 2.2 Cambridge in the regional context

was net immigration, comprising young families and retired people.

2.5 Associated with the immigration and population growth was expansion of the region's manufacturing industry. This expansion was remarkable, not just because East Anglia had been only modestly industrialised to start with; it was also the only region to record at least up to the mid-1970s an absolute gain in manufacturing employment whereas all other regions experienced losses, in some cases substantial.

2.6 The single most important component of East Anglia's manufacturing growth, until the mid-late 1970s, was establishment of factories by firms located in London in particular and also elsewhere in the South East. More often than not the move involved a complete relocation of the entire business and not just establishment of a subsidiary operation, a reversal of the typical pattern for industrial movement into the more distant assisted regions. Another distinctive feature of industrial migration into East Anglia has been the relatively small size of the establishments involved, in keeping with the size of the local labour markets throughout the region. Several factors underlay the industrial movement: amongst the 'push' factors was the drive to escape the congestion of the London area; and amongst the 'pull' factors were low wages and limited unionisation in East Anglia, which were a consequence chiefly of the historic dominance of agriculture as an employer.

2.7 During the 1970s an additional component of growth started becoming evident: indigenous formation of entirely new enterprises. A survey of manufacturing firms in this category in the 1971–81 period has shown that East Anglia, and Cambridgeshire in particular, fared particularly well by UK standards in terms of new firm formation (11).

2.8 Within East Anglia the distribution of growth has followed a clear pattern. It was initially concentrated in the south and south west of the region, essentially because of road and rail proximity to London – with the Ouse Valley (Huntingdon, St Neots) and Bury St Edmunds–Thetford areas (see map 2.2) being the principal areas of growth. There was also expansion in but mostly around the four largest towns (Cambridge, Ipswich, Norwich and Peterborough, the last becoming an increasingly significant growth point in the north

west in the 1970s following its designation as a new town in 1967). Cambridgeshire showed by far the highest formation rate of new manufacturing firms in the region.

2.9 Interestingly, again in marked contrast to the record of development of most other British regions in the post-war period, improvements to the transport system were made only a good while after the region's rapid growth had commenced and the development pattern established. The first motorway to serve the region directly – the M11 from north east of London to just north of Cambridge on the west side – was completed only in 1979. Similarly other strategic road improvements, such as the east-west dual carriageway A45 linking the increasingly important east coast ports (especially Felixstowe and Harwich) to East Anglia's hinterland and indeed the Midlands, were finished only around the same time. While some areas are now well served by rail, material improvements to the speed and quality of service connecting London with several important centres, notably Cambridge, have even now still to take place. It is noteworthy too that the region's growth proceeded despite the absence of ready access to an airport of any scale or direct international connections.

2.10 Norwich is the regional capital of East Anglia derived from its having been in mediaeval times at the centre of a prosperous grain and wool economy with substantial exports to mainland Europe. Before the industrialisation of Britain in the last century, Norwich had been by far the most important city in the region and indeed was the third largest city in England after London and Bristol. But despite some industrialisation notably in food and leather processing, and also in office services, Norwich's relative position in the region has declined this century. This is mainly a consequence of the long east-west lines of communication in East Anglia combined with the strong, independent growth of centres on the west of the region (Cambridge, Huntingdon, Peterborough) that have few natural links with Norwich and increasingly look elsewhere (principally London) for supply of special services. Each of the region's four main centres – Cambridge, Norwich, Ipswich, Peterborough – serves an important sub-regional market for shopping and other purposes, and has a widespread labour market catchment area. The growth of higher-level business and other services in Cambridge, however, combined with its prestige and proximity to London, is causing it steadily to emerge as the most important city in the region.

2.11 Overall, by UK standards East Anglia has sustained a remarkable record of growth over the past two decades and its prosperity has risen accordingly. Gross domestic product per head was fourth highest of all the regions in 1981 (having been eighth only five years before), and the rate of unemployment has generally been some 20% below the national average and second lowest of all the regions. The unemployment rate in Cambridgeshire has been even lower – about 40% below the national average (though there are parts of the county such as Peterborough and Wisbech where the rate has been well above the national average). The rate in Cambridge itself has consistently been even lower, at less than 50% of the national average.

THE COUNTY AND LOCAL CONTEXT

2.12 Developments in Cambridgeshire have mirrored in many ways the wider regional experience, growth pressures being greatest in the south of the county and in the Cambridge area. There were, however, quite distinctive features, most of them revolving around the special circumstances of Cambridge itself.

2.13 Up to about the mid-nineteenth century Cambridge was a university and market town and, more recently in the period, a regional rail centre. In the second half of the century, substantial growth started taking place; the population at the turn of the century was approaching 50 000, having been about 20 000 in 1830. Part of this was due to expansion of the University itself, as a result of greater liberality in undergraduate admissions policy (in common with other universities elsewhere) and of outstanding scientific and medical developments taking place in the Cavendish and other laboratories. Part was also due to the beginnings of modern industrial development.

2.14 A variety of developments took place consonant with Cambridge's role as a market and railway centre: for instance a jam factory (Chivers) was opened in 1873, just north of the city, and a flour mill (then Fosters now Dalgetys) was opened towards the end of the century at the railway station. Other industrial changes reflected rather more the university character of the town; there was expansion in the local printing and publishing industry and in paper-making nearby, and a sports goods business was started in 1855 by H J

Gray who was the rackets coach at St John's College. Both these industries have thrived, and the prominent local names in them – Cambridge University Press (itself now 400 years old), Heffers and Spicers in the former, and Grays – are famous worldwide.

2.15 In the context of this study, two developments were of very special significance. First, in 1881 the Cambridge Scientific Instrument Company (now Cambridge Instruments) was formed by Horace Darwin, a member of the University and son of the eminent naturalist Charles Darwin. The company was set up specifically to design and manufacture scientific equipment for the University but diversified successfully into other educational and industrial apparatus and worldwide markets. The company soon became widely recognised for the quality of its precision engineering and its apprentice training scheme and skilled craftsmen, and was one of the founders of the British instruments industry. A remarkable early record was established by way of invention and production of new instruments, including the world's first seismograph and commercial automatic temperature controller, much of the work being done in close association with the University. This record has continued, even if somewhat unevenly; among the most important recent developments was the 1950s–1960s collaboration between the company and the University engineering department on transmission and scanning electron microscope technology (see chapter 5).

2.16 Second, in 1896 W G Pye, who had served his apprenticeship at the Scientific Instrument Company, left his position as chief mechanic at the University's physics laboratory (the Cavendish) to establish his own firm to design and produce specialised laboratory equipment for scientific and educational purposes. The Pye group has similarly had a distinguished record of scientific achievements. Among them are pioneering development of radio and television technology, radar and other detection systems and also medical instruments in the inter-war period, and of hi-fi systems and telecommunications technology and analytical instruments after the second world war. In the 1930s the company worked very closely with the University supplying special equipment for such leading researchers as Rutherford, Adrian and Bernal.

2.17 Both Cambridge Instruments and the Pye Group (which now comprises two separate groups, Cambridge

BOX 2.1 UNIVERSITY OF CAMBRIDGE

It is not uncommon for tourists, unless standing in such obvious places as King's Parade, to be heard asking ". . . but where exactly is the University?" If its physical presence is not easily identified, then what actually makes it tick is infinitely harder.

Some of the basic facts are quite simple. The University's origins can be traced back at least to the late thirteenth century; the oldest college, Peterhouse, celebrated its seventh century in 1984. It is a large university by UK standards: an average load of some 12 160 full-time equivalent students in the first three years of the present decade (an increase of about 14% over the previous 15 years). Postgraduates make up about 21% of the total student population. Courses are offered by 62 different faculties and departments, 29 science-based and 33 arts based; in addition there are innumerable specialist research units mostly in the sciences. In terms of total student numbers the arts : science ratio has averaged 51 : 49 in recent years (over the past decade, as part of the commitment to maintain Cambridge "as a major scientific university" it has been a declared policy to move from a 55 : 45 towards a 50 : 50 balance and at least to keep the science share in the 48–52% range).

The University's excellence in science can be illustrated by reference to many individual pieces of research or the work of many departments, but probably the best example is the physics department (Cavendish laboratory) because of its long and distinguished record. It was endowed in 1870 and at once attracted a stream of scientists who were already or soon entered the forefront of their particular fields. In the period up to the 1930s physicists in the Cavendish were responsible for many of the major breakthroughs in atomic structure and crystal structure; in the second world war Cavendish scientists played leading roles in development of radar, telecommunications and electronics; and after the war the laboratory led the world again by applying physics in two totally new fields, molecular biology and radioastronomy. The Cavendish also played a vital role after the war in development of electron-optical analytical techniques which, in conjunction with work in the engineering department, led to design and construction of major new scientific equipment by local industry (see chapter 5).

The University is organised on collegiate as well as faculty/departmental lines. The colleges, of which there are currently 31, are autonomous and financially independent bodies; a few are very wealthy institutions in their own right. (The University itself is reasonably well endowed but like other universities depends on the national

University Grants Committee for funding of the recurrent expenditure of the faculties and departments; it has not escaped the recent rounds of cuts in UGC expenditure.) The University is in effect a loose federation of faculties and colleges.

Administration of the academic programme of the University is vested in the general board of the faculties. The vice chancellor is the senior officer but, since the position rotates every two years, the permanent administrative staff provide long-term continuity and exercise considerable influence. The recently retired secretary general of the faculties, Dr Ian Nicol, was secretary of the Mott committee (when he was secretary of the council of the school of physical sciences) and subsequently played a central role in shaping the administration's low-profile but positive attitudes towards links with industry.

The collegiate structure of the University has many important ramifications. Each college in effect forms a community, where people from many different disciplines and backgrounds can have an informal social exchange in a way that is qualitatively different from that in the departments (which are based on the same discipline) and that tends also to command a high degree of social loyalty. The college bursars typically play a crucial role in forming links between this community and the outside business world, both locally and beyond. The number and strength of the colleges together reinforce the decentralised structure of the University and emphasise the devolution of responsibility to the individual.

Many college fellows hold teaching or research positions in the University. Many of the more senior fellows play an important role in the University's various committees. Likewise, the heads and other senior members of the faculties and departments will all have college attachments. So, while in a formal sense the University and the colleges are separate entities, in practice there are innumerable interconnections which revolve around individuals simultaneously holding positions of influence in different parts of the overall structure.

The University and colleges have a far-reaching impact on many aspects of the city's economic and social life. Not only are they substantial owners of land in and around Cambridge, which results in their directly influencing patterns of physical development; they are sizeable employers – a 1977 estimate was that there were 7 000 full-time employees (of which 3 000 were teaching, research and technical staff). The University and college buildings and their grounds are a major tourist attraction, resulting in over £100 million of income to the city in 1983.

Electronic Industries and a set of subsidiaries of the Dutch-based Philips group) have experienced varying fortunes and a complex history of corporate changes over the years (which make fascinating stories in their own right, not least because of the lessons for business management and governmental intervention in industrial . restructuring). Their continuing presence has played a profoundly important part in the Cambridge phenomenon, and their strength today is of great consequence to the prosperity of the area.

2.18 New developments occurred in the city in the first part of this century to add to the success and growth of these two companies. The University continued expanding in many directions, notably with the physics and biochemistry departments each leading the world in several fields of research. A number of specialist research institutions grew up based on the local agricultural sector and in several cases closely linked to or part of the University. Among these were the internationally renowned Plant Breeding Institute (established in 1912), National Institute of Agricultural Botany (1919), Institute of Animal Physiology (1948) which in 1976 absorbed the Institute of Animal Nutrition (1949), and Houghton Poultry Research Station (1948).

2.19 Further industrial development occurred too. In 1934 a new company called Aero Research (now part of the Swiss company Ciba Geigy) was started in Duxford by N A de Bruyne, a spin-out from the Cavendish, to manufacture synthetic resins. In 1939 agrochemicals started being made in Harston by Pest Control Limited which has since become the Fisons Boots Company, now owned by the German Schering group. Also, the University and various of the local companies, notably Pye, played important roles in both world wars; Marshalls – the local aircraft engineering and vehicles company with whom de Bruyne had collaborated on development of the Mosquito aircraft – also played a significant part in the second world war effort; and in that war the city itself took on a new role as a regional base for certain departments of central government.

2.20 Associated with these developments was continuing growth in the local population. By 1951 the population of the city itself had reached nearly 90 000, and that of the so-called 'inner ring' of villages nearly 19 000. Revealingly, some 20% of the total population of about 108 000 were thought to have been new immigrants in the previous two decades.

2.21 This growth and especially the industrialisation were not universally welcomed in Cambridge. Physical development pressures were most keenly felt in the urban area and immediately surrounding villages, whereas the rural hinterland was declining. Consequently there was a fear that the traditional character of Cambridge – in which the University was the dominant influence, both in terms of a special way of life and of an architectural heritage that made the city centre one of unrivalled beauty – was being threatened. There was correspondingly a feeling that industrial growth, if it had to happen, should be channelled outside Cambridge. The development of the motor car industry at Cowley on the outskirts of Oxford was pointed to as indicative of the disharmonious impact of industry on a university town.

2.22 These fears in Cambridge coincided with a wider concern, at national level, about the whole system of physical planning and control and the ability of local government to implement it effectively. Lewis Silkin – who had been closely involved in the thinking that underlay the early 1940s plans for decentralisation from London and was appointed the first minister of the new department of town and country planning in the first post-war Labour government – took a particularly keen interest in Cambridge because his sons had been students at Trinity College. He was very keen to ensure that if at all possible the special character of Cambridge should be protected; and it was partly for this reason that planning powers were vested in the county council rather than the city council because it was felt that the former would be better able to manage the whole planning process.

2.23 This concern, local as well as national, found expression in the establishment of a special team under William Holford to prepare a city plan for Cambridge. This team, financed principally by the county council and set up with sympathetic endorsement from central government, was housed within the county's new planning department. Half of the latter's staff were assigned full-time to Holford, and were re-absorbed when Holford's work was completed. Thus although Holford acted independently, there was a close working relationship with the planning authority as well as an in-built element of continuity of thinking in the approach to planning the physical development of the city.

2.24 The starting point of Holford's influential report, published in 1950, was that Cambridge should remain predominantly a university town, of national importance and international reputation. While the broader role of Cambridge as a sub-regional centre was recognised, the explicit concern was that continuation of the post-1930s' pace and pattern of growth would irrevocably damage those qualities that made Cambridge such a special place.

2.25 Consequently Holford put forward proposals to reduce the rate of growth of the city and the immediately surrounding ring of villages and to permit expansion of the next ring of villages as well as to encourage growth of more distant market towns as a basis for revitalising the rural areas. The plan expressly proposed that industrial expansion in and near Cambridge should be limited and that large-scale production activities be discouraged from establishing anywhere in the county.

2.26 The Holford report was endorsed by central government in 1954; the change of administration in 1951 had not affected the basic thinking in Whitehall about the need for tight planning controls in Cambridge. Later in the decade the principle of containing the city's growth was reinforced by the drawing of a 'green belt' quite closely around the urban limits of Cambridge and the first ring of villages. In the early 1960s there was a further reinforcement when a tighter definition was adopted jointly by central and local government towards permissible industrial activity in the Cambridge area. Industrial development certificates became a powerful tool of control and new projects (or expansion of existing establishments) involving increases of more than five manufacturing employees were in general frowned upon.

2.27 The first formal review of the Holford plan was published in 1965. It acknowledged that some 'surplus' growth had taken place despite the restrictive policies, although less than there would have been without the policies, and that the pressures for growth remained seemingly unabated. (It was estimated that in 1963 the population of the city had reached 96 000 and that of the inner ring of villages 25 000, increases of 7% and 37% respectively compared with 1951.) The review concluded that Holford's approach should continue to guide planning policies, and indeed should be more tightly applied in the villages within a seven-mile radius

of Cambridge. To help relieve the pressure, the review provided for expansion of Sawston on the south side of the city and for the building of a new industrial and residential settlement at Bar Hill on the north.

2.28 Already in the 1950s and early 1960s the restrictive planning policies were having a discernible effect on the location of industry. For instance, Tube Investments had wished to establish its new R&D laboratories right in Cambridge because of its very close connections with the University's physics and engineering departments; but this was disallowed and instead the laboratories were set up in Hinxton Hall some 10 miles south of the city. Also, a number of smaller projects, notably some involving members of the engineering department, never sought to get started in Cambridge at all and instead set up elsewhere especially in London.

2.29 The even stricter application of planning policies by the county council in the mid-late 1960s resulted in a number of decisions which prompted considerable local controversy. Famous amongst them was a refusal to grant permission to IBM to establish its European research and development laboratories in Cambridge. There were other cases, too. Metals Research (a company established in 1957 by the Coles brothers, one of whom was a post-doctoral spin-out from the University's metallurgy department) and what is now PA Technology (formed in 1969 as a spin-out from Cambridge Consultants) were both denied permission to expand in Cambridge itself where they were already based. They both wished to remain in the Cambridge area and relocated to Melbourn. Similarly, Prosser Scientific Instruments were compelled to leave Cambridge, and set up in Hadleigh in Suffolk.

2.30 In retrospect these decisions can clearly be seen as going against the 'natural' trend of what was happening in Cambridge. Apart from the business developments mentioned above, there were other companies (notably Cambridge Consultants in 1960 and Applied Research of Cambridge in 1969) being formed 'spontaneously' in the same period. Clive Sinclair also formed a connection with the city which later became his company base. In addition, the University was continuing to expand and its research reputation was growing in major new fields such as molecular biology and computer applications notably in architectural and engineering design. Furthermore, central government had established a new national technological facility in Cambridge in the late 1960s, the Computer Aided Design Centre (see box 2.2). And in addition to the agricultural research laboratories mentioned earlier, which flourished, new laboratories were established in medical and related fields (such as the Medical Research Council laboratory of molecular biology and the independent charitable Strangeways laboratory specialising in the biochemical processes involved in rheumatoid arthritis and associated problems in skeletal biology.

2.31 It was not only with hindsight that the planning decisions were regarded as at variance with the basic trends and indeed the needs of the area. The University's previously negative attitude to the growth of Cambridge had gradually become more relaxed and there was a rising awareness of the potential benefits to itself of the city's becoming a prosperous regional centre. There was, too, concern growing in the University about the implications, for its own financing and long-term development, of the early 1960s shift in national education policy which directed all general development funds into the new technological universities and other higher educational establishments.

2.32 Moreover, amongst key individuals in the University's laboratories and research institutes there was at that time a perception that the vitality and relevance of their own work would be dependent on there being in the vicinity of the University a good number and diversity of industrial and other non-academic research establishments. They sensed that in the long term industry would be an important source of research funding. Most important of all, they believed that increasingly in the future their research students would have to find careers in industry rather than in academic institutions. It would be far easier for these developments to take place if science-based industry were well established in the area: they were well aware of what was happening at other academic centres elsewhere, notably Stanford and MIT, and saw the benefits that were flowing from such activities.

2.33 In response to the lobbying by these individuals (who mostly came from the physics and engineering departments) and against a background of central government exhortations about the need for society to realise the benefits of 'the white hot technological revolution', the University authorities decided to act.

In July 1967 they set up a sub-committee of the senate to 'consider in greater detail and advise on the planning aspects of the relationship between the University and science-based industry'. Formation of this sub-committee was supported by the Cambridge city council, which had for some while felt frustrated by what it regarded as the county council's artificial ceiling on its employment and rates base. The city council (on which at that time the University was automatically represented) had come under Labour Party control in the mid-1960s, and this greatly increased the commitment to employment and industry compared with the earlier Tory-dominated council (and also the Tory-controlled county council). The University's sub-committee was, interestingly, also strongly backed by some of the major local employers who were experiencing recruitment difficulties which they argued resulted from unwarranted restrictions on provision of housing.

2.34 The report of the University sub-committee – known as the Mott report after the chairman, Professor Sir Nevill Mott, who was head of the Cavendish – was completed in November 1968, approved by the senate in July 1969 and published in October 1969 (22). That the work of the sub-committee took so long is significant. It involved a long process of consultations, as well as many rounds of debate and lobbying, both inside and outside the University. In this sense the published report represented a critical stage in a lengthy process – in effect that a degree of consensus had been reached among the University and local planning authorities – rather than simply the deliberations and recommendations of an exclusively University group.

2.35 The sub-committee's report addressed directly the need 'to strengthen the interaction between teaching and scientific research on the one hand and its application in industry, medicine and agriculture on the other', and concluded that 'the root of the problems' on which it had been engaged lay in the 'Holford principles . . . which were formulated on the basis of population forecasts well below those . . . generally accepted and a rate of University development smaller than (had) in fact taken place'. The report observed that the ensuing planning restrictions had not only created difficulties of recruitment for the University but had also imposed even more severe restrictions on industrial and other forms of growth not directly connected with the University.

BOX 2.2 ORIGINS OF THE COMPUTER AIDED DESIGN CENTRE

The Labour administration that took office in 1964 carried as one of its banners the economic and social benefits of the 'white heat of technology'. A number of special projects and new policies promoting this concept were conceived in the heady early years of the administration in which powerful individuals like P M S Blackett were very closely involved. He had been at the Cavendish in the 1920s and 1930s when the breakthroughs on atomic structure were made, had played a leading scientific role at the Admiralty in the war, had subsequently become president of the Royal Society and in the early 1960s along with others was becoming increasingly concerned that the brilliant technological achievements of the war years had not been carried over into civilian and industrial life.

One of the major concerns of the day was to bring together the disciplines of mechanical engineering and electronics/computing (there were several major companies very strong in one or other, but none in both). In the early-mid 1960s the concepts of computer aided design (CAD) began to emerge and Ieuan Maddock (chief scientist at the Ministry of Technology later the Department of Trade & Industry, who had long worked closely with Blackett) chaired a national committee on the subject, and the decision was taken to establish a national CAD facility. Consideration was given to three main options: creating a new public sector establishment, giving a contract to the private sector (International Computers and Tabulators – ICT later ICL) or putting a facility in a university. Eventually a hybrid was adopted: government funded, located alongside a university and managed on contract by ICL.

Cambridge was selected as a location for four chief reasons:

(a) CAD then required very large computing capacity. It was necessary to select a British machine rather than the American Univac, but the options were limited. Fortunately an Atlas 2 machine happened to be available for installation in Cambridge;

(b) Cambridge University's computing specialisation lay in applications, which was highly appropriate compared with the emphasis on hardware at Manchester (the only other university in contention);

(c) Maurice Wilkes at the Cambridge computing

laboratory had recently set up a strong CAD group under Charles Lang who had been recruited back from MIT (see boxes 2.2 and 4.3);

(d) John Baker, head of the University's engineering department, was an enthusiastic supporter of the idea, and the University administration was generally very positive (the Centre became the first tenant on the University's High Cross site on the western outskirts of Cambridge, taking occupation of premises surplus to the Cavendish laboratory's needs).

The hybrid character of the CADCentre never worked wholly satisfactorily. Similarly, it proved impossible under the organisation and management arrangements properly to reconcile the several objectives of being an R&D centre and a technology transfer agency as well as achieving financial independence from government.

Despite these difficulties the Centre attracted staff of outstanding calibre and truly leading edge work was carried out. In the early years there was close collaboration with the University computer laboratory and engineering department, and also with young local companies like Applied Research of Cambridge.

There was a growing conviction among some of the Centre's staff that exciting opportunities for commercial application of their know-how could not and would not be exploited by the Centre. Combined with a prolonged period of uncertainty in the mid-1970s concerning the Centre's status and possibly even its survival, this frustration caused some of the leading individuals to spin out to set up their own local company Cambridge Interactive Systems which has been highly successful (see box 3.3). The Centre is estimated to be one of the most significant sources of spin-out firms in Cambridge though more recently this has happily not been because of the strength of the 'push' factor.

In the late 1970s the Centre began to be rationalised and put on a more business-like footing. It was privatised in 1983 and operates now as CADCentre Limited and is itself proving successful commercially. The shareholders in the new venture are ICL, WS Atkins (engineering consultants), SIA (computer bureau, London-based subsidiary of a French organisation), Cambridge University and Trinity and St John's Colleges.

2.36 In looking ahead the Mott report concluded that it would be strongly in the combined and separate interests of the county, city and University to encourage a limited growth of existing and new science-based industry and other applied research units in and near Cambridge. It recommended that ways be found of creating a 'science park' in the Cambridge area which would offer the right physical and planning environment for science-based industry and would be accessible to University departments.

2.37 Though hard won the response to the Mott report from the county authorities was, when it came, positive and forward-looking. A review of the county development plan as it bore on Cambridge was published early in 1971; a principal reason for its being undertaken was to deal with Mott's recommendations. This review did not question the basic aims and policies of the Holford plan but, following extensive consultations in the area, stated emphatically that 'bona fide science-based industry' was considered desirable and appropriate to Cambridge and would be encouraged on properly located sites. The review endorsed the view that the vitality of the University, itself so essential to Cambridge, would depend in part on its outside links; and it foresaw the benefits of encouraging new R&D-oriented industry to establish and grow ("to a reasonable extent") especially where there existed the potential for fruitful links with existing firms in the area. The 1971 review also allowed rather more freedom for development of service industries and offices in Cambridge, particularly in relation to its role as a sub-regional centre.

2.38 This rather more positive attitude towards development generally set the tone for both the county's and city's planning policies through the 1970s and up to the present. These attitudes were reinforced by local government reorganisation in 1974 – relations between the city and county councils improved greatly as a result partly of a change-round of senior planning and other officers. Also the incorporation into the county of Huntingdonshire (with its high unemployment around Peterborough) had the effect of making the planners more conscious of the need for policies conducive to employment growth. These latter concerns were not directed at Cambridge itself, which has always had low unemployment, but nevertheless there was a heightened awareness in a period of recession of the impact of local policies on economic development.

2.39 The Mott report is widely and justifiably regarded in Cambridge today as constituting a watershed in the evolution of the University's official attitude to industrial development and to collaboration with the local authorities. It was almost certainly without precedent in Britain at the time that a university should take the lead so explicitly and forcefully in such planning matters – it is still highly unusual even today. The fact of Cambridge University's doing so thus carried special weight. The report led directly to establishment by Trinity College of the Cambridge science park (see chapter 4) and, as expressed in a major 1974 report on the University's long-term future, to the University authorities' positive attitudes towards having science-based industrial tenants on its own land. Subsequent developments at High Cross on the west of Cambridge, at the New Addenbrookes Hospital site in the south and at various redundant premises elsewhere in the city, fall into this latter category.

2.40 The Mott committee's report, and all the deliberations and argument that went with it, indirectly had a profoundly important long-term influence on the academic community. This was because the process of preparing the document helped clarify the distinction between 'smoke-stack' and 'science-based' industry and legitimised the role of the latter as an integral element in the future of the University's research and the Cambridge scene more generally. The positive attitudes towards industrial involvement found today in the University administration, and reasonably widely in the academic community, have been shaped by many factors but the Mott committee stands out as probably the single most important among them.

2.41 The Mott committee's positive attitudes to industrial development must not be taken as an indication that the attitude of the University authorities moved unreservedly in favour of uncontrolled growth of Cambridge as a city. The 1974 report on the future size and structure of the University referred to earlier concluded that, while there would have to be some further increase in the number of student places, the "unique character of Cambridge would be changed irrevocably by an indefinite expansion" and that the University should plan its development accordingly. There were then, and still remain, powerful moderating influences on growth and change in Cambridge.

2.42 That the Mott committee was convened and had such a long-term impact was in part a reflection of the research activity that was then going on in the laboratories of the University and associated research institutes. Several of these research fields had significant industrial application, whether existing or potential, and three in particular are relevant to this study: computing, scanning electron microscopy and associated surface analytical and electron optical techniques, and the biosciences spanning both agriculture and medicine. Chapter 5 will discuss the contribution of this research to the development of high technology industry in Cambridge; the important point here is that in the late 1960s and early 1970s there was in the local research laboratories a strongly developing sense of, or actual involvement in, industrial application.

2.43 Finally in setting the scene for later chapters, note must be taken of one particular development that took place at the end of the 1970s. During the 1970s there was a rising incidence in Cambridge of new, high technology firm formation, most of them engaged in computing (and many located in the Jesus Lane – Thompson's Lane area in the centre of the city). The presence of these firms passed largely unnoticed until 1979 when several of them got together to form the Cambridge Computer Group (see box 5.3 in chapter 5) in order to promote their joint interests. It was the existence of this group, even though it remained highly informal, that drew attention locally to the emerging phenomenon and, as explained later, led the way to Barclays Bank playing such an important role in stimulating new high technology company formation in the ensuing years.

CONCLUDING COMMENTS

2.44 A number of broad observations – to be elaborated in later chapters – can be made at this stage. First, there is a long history – now a little over one hundred years – of high technology companies setting up in Cambridge as a direct result of the presence of the University. The current phenomenon of company formation may be different in frequency and scale but not in basic kind.

2.45 Second, the unique character of Cambridge as a city has itself exercised a special influence. There are many ingredients to this: the dominant role of the University and the colleges in the city's long-term development, physical and otherwise, and the strength of the University in key scientific fields; the limited extent of previous industrialisation, and the absence of traditional industry and large companies that might otherwise have been dominant; and the growing emergence of Cambridge as a significant urban centre in a region that was itself experiencing rapid growth and prosperity.

2.46 Third, it would be an easy but simplistic and misplaced criticism to condemn the thinking that underlay the Holford plan and ensuing planning policies as inimical to Cambridge's long-term interest as a University and particularly as a prospering local economy. The fact is that Cambridge's architectural heritage and its cultural and social life are unique, and the way they interact is itself unique. Excessive growth or growth of the wrong kind could too easily damage these qualities. The lasting contribution of the Holford plan, even if it would itself have preferred a more conservative approach, was two-fold. First, it ensured that policies of reasonable restraint on growth would be adopted in the long term; it thereby gave Cambridge what must be seen as constructive guidelines for taking new economic opportunities as they arose and adapting physically to new development. And second, by preventing any individual or general large-scale developments to take place which would have put enormous pressure on the labour market and on the area's physical capacity, it made it easier for small firms to start up and grow. In this way it indirectly led to encouragement of scientific and technological, rather than production, activities in which, as will be seen, Cambridge's long-term comparative advantage lies.

2.47 Fourth, the issues raised by the Holford and Mott reports remain highly relevant to the continuing development of Cambridge; even more so, precisely because of their success. In particular, to anticipate later arguments, the substantial growth of high technology industry (and of other sectors in the city's economy) that has taken place over the past decade and the further growth in prospect continue to present major challenges to orderly management of the area's development and to retention of Cambridge's special character.

2.48 Finally, this chapter has essentially sought to describe the 'incubation period' of the substantial growth of high technology industry that has taken place in Cambridge over the past decade or so. But it is helpful to anticipate briefly the material presented in the next and later chapters, and to indicate briefly the scale and nature of this growth. We identified a total of 322 high technology firms in the Cambridge area by the end of 1984 (with perhaps a further 25 in existence but as yet unidentified); of these three quarters were indigenous and independent. Only 25 years before there was a total of 30 companies, and 10 years before around 100. Employment in these companies now accounts for some 17% of total employment in the Cambridge travel-to-work area.

2.49 Moreover, among the companies formed in the past decade are some that have become household names in Britain (Sinclair Research and Acorn Computers, mostly but not only because of their dominant position in the national microcomputer market). And there are others that, even if less well known to the general public, are among the world's leaders in their particular technologies and markets. These are notably in computer aided design, specialised hardware and software design and development, scientific instrumentation (electron optics, vacuum technology and surface analysis being areas of particular strength), image processing, ink-jet printing and increasingly in the biosciences. Altogether the companies span an impressive range of technology and are creating an 'effervescent' and dynamic business culture in Cambridge.

3

CAMBRIDGE HIGH TECHNOLOGY COMPANIES — 1:
A STATISTICAL PICTURE

INTRODUCTION

3.1 This chapter presents the main statistical results of our interviews with high technology companies in the Cambridge area, as explained in chapter 1 and appendix C. This quantitative picture of the Cambridge phenomenon covers 261 firms which we were able to interview successfully. We estimate that these firms accounted for some 85% of the firms in the phenomenon overall in mid-1984 (which was when our main statistical survey was completed), and for an even higher proportion of output and employment.*

3.2 Much of the chapter describes quantitatively the size and structure of the phenomenon in a variety of dimensions. The overall picture that starts emerging is clear, but lacks life; and in order to start giving a better feel of what really makes up the Cambridge high technology scene, thumbnail sketches of eight of the companies (the six who supported the study plus two others chosen reasonably randomly) are included in this chapter and the next.

TIME PROFILE AND AGE STRUCTURE

3.3 Figure 3.1, which charts the time profile of establishment of the 261 firms, clearly shows a significant increase in births in the 1960s followed by an 'explosion' starting in the early-middle 1970s.

*Appendix C explains how the estimates of the number of firms in the phenomenon were arrived at.

3.4 If the sheer number of companies is striking, then their youthfulness is even more so. Fully 60% of the population was established after 1978; on another measure, about 190 of the enterprises set up in the area in the decade 1974–1984. These data may be contrasted with an estimate of 250 new high technology firms started in the 1960s on the San Francisco peninsula (4). Even if the Cambridge data are confined to spin-outs and also an attempt is made to allow for the definition of high technology firms adopted in the San Francisco study, the corresponding numbers of Cambridge companies started in the past decade is of the order of 100, which is still sizeable given the substantial differences in population of the two areas.

3.5 In the 20 years since 1964 the number of companies establishing operations in the Cambridge area has averaged nearly one per month; in the past 10 years the monthly rate has been just over $1\frac{1}{2}$. The peak years have been 1981 ($2\frac{1}{2}$ per month) and 1983 (just under 3 per month). The data for 1984 are obviously incomplete; our guess is somewhere around 2 per month. The average annual birth rate (new operations established in a year as a percentage of the number of companies, surviving to 1984, in operation at the start of the year) has been 11.4% over the 20-year period from 1964 and 11.8% over the past 10 years. The peak birth rate so far has been a little over 20% (in 1978).

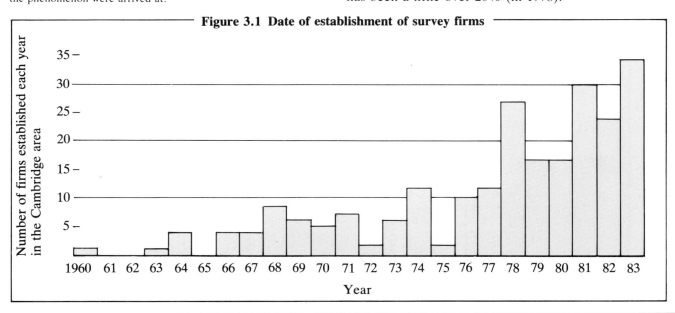

Figure 3.1 Date of establishment of survey firms

Number of firms established each year in the Cambridge area

1960 61 62 63 64 65 66 67 68 69 70 71 72 73 74 75 76 77 78 79 80 81 82 83

Year

BOX 3.1   ACORN COMPUTER GROUP PLC

Acorn Computers has been one of the most success-ful high technology firms in Cambridge to have moved swiftly from start-up to volume production of standard-ised items, and also to have combined leading edge technological excellence with an overriding commitment to the market.

As is well known, the company has had phenom-enal growth since its establishment in December 1978. At the time of start-up only the two founders were involved; now there are over 400 staff. Turnover has grown from £30 000 in the first year to approximately £90m in 1984. The company was taken successfully to the stock market at the end of 1983.

The founders were Hermann Hauser and Chris Curry. Hauser had been engaged in physics research in the University's Cavendish laboratory, but had become especially interested in computer applications and after doing part-time consultancy was actively looking for more serious business opportunities; Chris Curry had been running a company called Science of Cambridge in association with Clive Sinclair. The two met and realised they jointly had the technological and market knowledge to establish a computer business, and in March 1978 set up a business called Cambridge Processor Unit to do this. They were later joined on a part-time basis by Andy Hopper of the University's computer laboratory, who had established with Hauser a company called Orbis to exploit commercially the Cambridge ring technology (a local area network) of which he (Hopper) had been the main inventor. Hauser and Curry remain the principal execu-tives in the company which is on a vastly different scale and nature compared with only a few years ago.

The University, the computer laboratory in par-ticular, remains important to Acorn. Somewhat over 50% of the 100 graduate employees are from Cambridge, and close research links flourish both formally and informally. Its original premises were a small office in the city centre; it now is located on the periphery of the city where it has been able to refurbish old buildings and put up new buildings and also has, subject to planning permission, room for substantial further expansion. The company has not found that being outside the centre of the city has damaged its links with the University.

Acorn's activities can be broadly described as the conceptualisation and design of microcomputers for home, educational and business purposes, local area networks, and associated hardware and software. It undertakes no large-scale manufacture and assembly itself, this being sub-contracted to other companies else-where in the UK. The decision to concentrate on develop-ing an in-house excellence in computing research, devel-opment and design was deliberate. It was felt that under-taking its own manufacturing would have unnecessarily inhibited the company's performance, especially by de-flecting management's attention from market development which was always seen as the key to long-term success.

The company's breakthrough into very rapid growth, after an initial period in which it produced and sold by mail order home computer kits, came with its winning an exclusive contract from the BBC to supply microcomputers for the purposes of an extensive television programme series the latter was undertaking. After a highly successful performance on this contract and despite stiff competition from other companies, Acorn has re-cently had its contract with the BBC renewed for four years. Acorn has also been one of the most prominent microcomputer businesses in the educational market.

Acorn has moved quickly over the past year or two to diversify its products and geographic markets as well as to develop wider interests. The company exports to 25 countries all over the world, and a special deal has been struck with the Government of India for the introduction of microcomputers into schools. It has also gained a significant stake in complementary hardware and software companies, and has entered into joint ventures with com-panies such as ICL and Racal. Its entry into the business computing market has been signalled by its acquisition and development of IBM compatible products.

Acorn has encountered and so far successfully weathered all the business problems of rapid growth. It has been notably successful in retaining an informal and intellectually lively corporate style and atmosphere with-out prejudice to developing an operational and strategic discipline to all aspects of its business. It has become a significant business presence in Cambridge: as an em-ployer, purchaser of specialist and other local supplies, investor in new business ventures and of course also as a national name that brings prestige to the city.

BOX 3.2 CAMBRIDGE CONSULTANTS LIMITED

CCL provides a fascinating example of an indigenous Cambridge company, launched in 1960 by a group of newly graduated scientists and engineers, that went through a long period of operational success but financial uncertainty and, after near disaster, has developed into one of the country's leading R&D contractors in the physical sciences. It has also exercised a distinctive influence on the Cambridge high technology business scene, directly through the number of companies it has helped spin out from itself and indirectly through its being regarded especially in its early days as indicative of the creativity and individual enterprise of the University's engineers and scientists.

The company was the brainchild of Tim Eiloart, but start-up also involved David Southward (now a director of Sinclair Research); one of the other founders was Roger Needham, who is now head of the University's computer laboratory. Among other individuals who played a key role in the development of the firm were Gordon Edge (who left in 1970 to set up what has become PA Technology on the Melbourn science park), and Richard Cutting who (after being CCL's chief executive from 1971 to 1983) is now head of Sinclair Research's Metalab in Cambridge.

The start-up objective was to sell high quality technical and design services to manufacturing industry, capitalizing explicitly on the Cambridge origins and connections of the company. Despite what with hindsight can best be described as business naivete, the company grew albeit haphazardly. It used the University and related national industrial networks to generate market leads and it recruited a variety of highly talented individuals some of whom perhaps too easily tended to do things that interested them without regard to commercial realities. The company developed a range of excellent electronics instruments in particular, but was unable fully to capitalise on their potential.

In the late 1960s a holding company (AIM Associates Cambridge Limited) was formed and CCL became one of its five subsidiaries (this involved no real change in the status and autonomy of CCL). The AIM group quite quickly ran into financial difficulties, and eventually in 1971 CCL was bought by Arthur D Little, the prestigious Boston-based R&D and consultancy firm.

The takeover by ADL proved a turning point for,

although CCL has throughout retained a high, almost total degree of autonomy, it has since that time achieved a business-like discipline and a sophistication that it lacked before. While concentrating on scientific and technical consultancy, CCL now has some 170 employees, nearly 100 of whom are graduates (about 40 with higher degrees). Around 20% of the graduates are from Cambridge. Its turnover is currently of the order of £5m.

Its markets are so far predominantly (80%) in the UK, the single most important sector being the defence industry though there is an increasing commitment to developing overseas more and a subsidiary company has been established in West Germany.

In its early years CCL occupied a number of small, more or less makeshift premises in the centre and then the suburbs of Cambridge before moving out to purpose-built but not entirely satisfactory premises in Bar Hill. Since 1979 it has occupied its own custom-designed and prestigious premises on the Cambridge science park. On the science park CCL is well recognised for the friendly and supportive role it plays in helping young, neighbour companies in a variety of ways such as allowing them the use of workshop facilities.

Despite its origins and original intentions, CCL has never developed especially close links with the University and currently makes little use of it. But a Cambridge location (reinforced by being on the science park) is valuable from a marketing viewpoint and because it is easy to recruit good people in and to the area.

CCL has been one of the more prolific sources of spin-out companies in the area (see the family tree shown in chapter 3). It has always encouraged people to 'do their own thing' if they so wished; even if their departure was initially a loss to CCL, on balance the net benefits accruing from spin-outs have been positive. Early in 1984 CCL decided to formalise its encouragement of new spin-out ventures by establishment of a division specifically for this purpose; assistance being given in whatever ways necessary, notably including commercialisation of technological ideas and provision of finance, in return for licence fees, royalties or equity participation. Towards the end of the year this division was itself spun out as a new enterprise, enabling it to offer its technology venture management services to the wider market and not just within CCL.

3.6 Data on the incidence of failures are not readily available. Local bank managers believe that death rates of small high technology firms have been low, and certainly significantly lower than for conventional firms. Our investigations suggest that there have perhaps been a total of up to 20 failures in the past five years, representing some 7% of the total existing stock of companies. This is a remarkably low figure – government statistics for all categories of small firms, based on VAT returns, show that within four years of start-up some 30–40% of firms can be expected to have failed. Low failure rates, though not as low as in Cambridge, appear also to be a feature of new high technology firms in the Boston area (17).

CORPORATE STATUS

3.7 A striking feature of the companies is the very high incidence of independent enterprises (three quarters of the total population) – see table 3.1. The great majority (88%) of all companies have not changed their corporate status since establishing in Cambridge, and only 4% have been acquired by or merged with other companies.

3.8 Of the 25% of firms classed as subsidiaries, a little over half (53%) had UK parents (see table 3.2). The USA was the second most important parent group (26%), followed by mostly European countries each with only a few cases. In the relatively few cases where corporate status had changed since start-up as a consequence of acquisition, the UK and USA were again the prominent countries of the company making the acquisition.

OUTPUT AND EMPLOYMENT

3.9 As table 3.3 shows, total employment in 1984 is an estimated 13 700 and output some £890 million – both relatively large figures. Because so many of the companies are very young, and also because a few of

the longer-established ones are very large (by Cambridge standards), it is interesting to identify separately the contributions to employment and output of the companies established since the birth rate started increasing rapidly (1974).

3.10 These data show the substantial contribution made by the companies established in the past decade: by 1984, some 3 800 jobs (just over a quarter of the total high technology jobs) and nearly £350 million turnover. Interestingly the companies established since 1979 are so numerous (128) that they have generated more jobs than those (61) established in the previous five-year period 1974–78. The aggregate turnover of this latter group, however, is very much larger chiefly because of the substantial growth of three companies (Sinclair, Acorn and CIS) founded between 1974 and 1978.

Table 3.1 Corporate status of companies, 1984

	Percentage
Independent	75
UK branch	2
UK subsidiary	11
Foreign subsidiary	12
	100

(No of companies in sample = 261)

Table 3.2 Companies' original basis of establishment in Cambridge

	Percentage
Independent new firm	73
Relocation of existing operation	9
New branch	2
New subsidiary	16
	100

(No of companies in sample = 261)

Table 3.3 1984 employment and turnover of different groups of companies

	No of companies	Employment No.	Turnover £m	Turnover/ person £000s
All companies	261	13 700	890	65
Companies estd in period 1974–78	61	1 750	242	138
Companies estd in period since 1979	128	2 030	102	50

BOX 3.3 CAMBRIDGE INTERACTIVE SYSTEMS LIMITED

CIS, one of the first and so far the most successful spin-out company from the Computer Aided Design Centre in Cambridge, is of special interest for two main reasons: the way it launched itself from a 'soft' start swiftly into market-led 'hardening', and the benefits it has derived from becoming a subsidiary of a major US corporation.

The company was started in 1977 by four of the leading people in the CADCentre: Tom Sancha (the present managing director), John Chilvers (who at present is 'on loan' to the CADCentre as its managing director following its recent privatisation), Dick Newell and Mike Williamson, of whom all except Newell were Cambridge graduates. They felt that their expertise in CAD, developed at the University and the Computer Aided Design Centre, had outstanding business potential and that the Centre, as a government research institution, was not the right vehicle for realising it. When in 1976 the Centre's future status became uncertain they decided to set up on their own. For cash flow reasons they phased their departure over a 10-month period, Sancha leaving first in March 1977.

The founders recognised that, although (and because) they were at the leading edge of CAD-CAM technology, it would take time to develop significant clients among their target group of large engineering and vehicles companies. Consequently, in the start-up period, they undertook a miscellany of consulting assignments (including graphics for TV commercials) to generate cash flow while simultaneously developing a variety of new products including one particular drafting system which became the core of their future products and services. As they started selling the latter, so they raised their consultancy prices: this had the intended effects of generating substantial additional cash for development purposes and, eventually, of pricing themselves out of the market. By the time the latter happened they were already well advanced in design and production of three-dimensional drafting systems in a number of different industries, and their clients included such prestigious names such as GEC, BMW and Hunting Engineering.

In 1979 CIS merged with AGS, another spin-out from the CADCentre that had set up in 1977 to market

CAD in Europe; they subsequently also gave an exclusive licence to Prime Computers (whose computers were integral to most of CIS's CAD systems) to sell outside Europe.

Growth was rapid: turnover had risen fifty-fold by 1981 (and a further six-fold since then, to reach some £30m in 1984). The company was split among several sites in Cambridge (having moved out of Sancha's home in 1978), and there was a growing need for consolidation not only in physical but also in management terms especially as their operations were increasingly becoming international. The need for capital to finance long-term expansion also became pressing. After considering a number of purely financing packages, the company decided to sell out entirely (through a share swap) to Computervision based in Bedford, Mass, which is one of the world's largest CAD companies. In this way although CIS and the Dutch marketing arm remain highly independent, they have secured access to substantial financial resources and particularly marketing, financial and management expertise which they could not otherwise have expected to achieve for many years.

CIS has gone through an exciting entrepreneurial phase, with a strong market orientation to its technological excellence. While their management systems have become more structured and sophisticated since the acquisition by Computervision, CIS remains committed to operating as informally as possible since it believes this provides the most fertile environment for its specialist staff.

CIS currently employs 70 people in Cambridge (14 with higher degrees) and 15 are graduates of Cambridge. There are few formal and operational links with the University but the company benefits in marketing and recruitment terms from the prestige of Cambridge, and there is continuing informal interaction with the academics and other CAD experts in the city. CIS has recently renovated and extended an old mill in Harston, a village about 6 miles south of Cambridge, on which all its UK operations are now based, and it sees this as providing an excellent long-term base for remaining closely involved with the high technology scene in Cambridge.

SIZE AND SIZE DISTRIBUTION

3.11 The bulk of the companies are small. This can be gauged from the mean and median data on the three time-groups of companies noted in the previous section, given in table 3.4.

Table 3.4 Company size, 1984

	Employment	Turnover (£m)
All companies		
Mean	53	3.4
Median	11	0.35
Total	13 700	890
Companies established in period 1974–78		
Mean	29	9.3
Median	13	0.6
Total	1 750	242
Companies established since 1979		
Mean	16	0.76
Median	8	0.3
Total	2 030	102

3.12 The skewed size distribution, with a heavy predominance of very small companies, can be measured in other ways. For instance, in 1984 almost 30% of the companies had five employees or fewer; 75% had 30 employees or less. Similarly, just over 40% of the companies have an estimated 1984 turnover of below £350,000 each.

GROWTH PERFORMANCE

3.13 We sought to measure the growth of the companies over the five-year period 1979–1984. The data we obtained were not wholly satisfactory because a good number of the companies could not remember their 1979 figures and also almost half of the sample were formed after 1979. Nevertheless, we have derived some information which shows the dynamism of the high technology sector.

3.14 In aggregate employment terms there was an increase of about 4 100 jobs (43%) over the period. The bulk of this (over 90%) was accounted for by firms established since 1974. In terms of compound growth, the average rate of employment increase of each company was about 15% per annum (31% per annum for companies started in the 1974–78 period); and again in compound terms, the average rate of increase in real output was 25% per annum for the whole group of companies and 41% for the 1974–78 starts.

INDUSTRIAL STRUCTURE

3.15 Table 3.5 gives the sectoral distribution of the companies in terms of numbers of companies, employment and turnover, appendix C explains the exact make-up of each sector.

3.16 It should be pointed out that classification of this kind is not so straightforward as might be expected. For instance, many companies undertake activities in more than one sector – a good example would be the computer software firms engaging also in consultancy. Our approach has been to assign a firm to that sector according to its dominant activity. Another complication lies in the description of firms in the computer hardware category; while technically correct, this might be taken as implying that they are involved in manufacture of hardware whereas in fact their principal activity is in research, design and development which on a different classification could put them in a software or services category. (It is for these reasons, among others, that the conventional distinction between the manufacturing and services sector is not particularly useful in high technology industry.)

Table 3.5 Sectoral distribution of companies, 1984

	No of companies %	Employment %	Turnover %
Chemicals/ biotechnology	4	9	15
Electrical equipment	3	2	2
Electronics capital goods	22	21	14
Other electronics	10	11	16
Instrument engineering	17	22	14
Computer hardware	11	7	23
Computer software	23	8	8
Consultancy/R&D	6	17	7
Other	4	3	1
	100	100	100
Total absolute value	261	13 700	£890m

3.17 The dominance on all counts of electronics, instrument engineering and computing is clearly evident. Perhaps the most striking feature of the data is the exceptionally high turnover of the computer hardware sector relative to its significance in terms of employment and numbers of companies. This can be gauged too from its output/employment ratio – £230 000/employee (1984 prices) compared with an average for the whole sample of £65 000/employee. The chief reason for these characteristics of the computer hardware section is that several companies concerned subcontract their volume production and assembly operations to businesses outside Cambridge.

GEOGRAPHIC LOCATION

3.18 The firms are heavily concentrated in what is known as the Cambridge sub-area and in particular in Cambridge itself (see map 3.1 and table 3.6). The sub-area accounts for some 80% of the phenomenon in terms both of numbers of companies and employment; the share of Cambridge itself is in the region of 50%. Further, about 17% of employment in the sub-area is in the high technology companies.

3.19 It is interesting to observe how spatial clustering can develop as a result of specific events or decisions. Thus, the concentration of firms in the St Ives and (to a lesser extent) Huntingdon areas derives in good measure from the period in the 1960s when Cambridge Consultants was located in St Ives; and the concentration in Melbourn is due principally to establishment there of PA Technology, Metals Research (since merged with Cambridge Instruments) and, most recently and importantly, of a science park.

COMPANY GENEALOGY

3.20 We have attempted to construct a 'family tree' of the companies, in order to give an indication of the inter-connectedness of local high technology business development. This tree, given in the separate chart between pages 32 and 33, shows two kinds of inter-organisational links:

(a) establishment in the area of a new company (in high technology itself or else supplying specialised services to high technology companies) in which the person(s) who played a major role in the founding process came *directly* from existing local high technology organisation(s) (which could be other companies, the University or other research laboratories). This is by far the most important kind of link in quantitative terms;

(b) formation of a new subsidiary, or incorporation of an existing local firm as a subsidiary, by a high technology company already in the area, in which the subsidiaries operate essentially as independent companies.

3.21 In addition to the 244 inter-connected businesses on the family tree, the chart also includes a list of Cambridge firms that are very much part of the phenomenon but that do not have links of the kinds described (whether 'parent' or 'child') with other local firms and organisations. This list thus includes companies that have moved into the area from outside. Another important category of companies on the list comprises those set up by Cambridge graduates or by people who had previously worked in local high technology organisations but who in both cases had a spell elsewhere before returning to Cambridge to set up in business.

3.22 Altogether there are 355 businesses shown on the chart (330 surviving), which may be compared with a total of 261 in our data bank. The chart has more companies on it for several reasons, the most important being that it includes companies that we did not interview fully and also we adopted a more liberal definition of eligibility for inclusion on the chart than in the data bank.

3.23 One of the distinctive features of the Cambridge high technology scene is the movement of key people (not only founders) between different organisations within the area, sometimes interrupted by experience elsewhere. This is understandable: 'people transfer' is universally recognised as the best form of technology

Table 3.6 Spatial distribution of the companies, 1984

	Nos of Companies		Employment	
	No	%	No	%
Cambridge city & science park	110	42	7 450	54
'Inner ring' villages	32	12	1 450	11
Rest of Cambridge sub-area	63	24	2 350	17
Outside Cambridge sub-area	56	22	2 450	18
Total	261	100	13 700	100

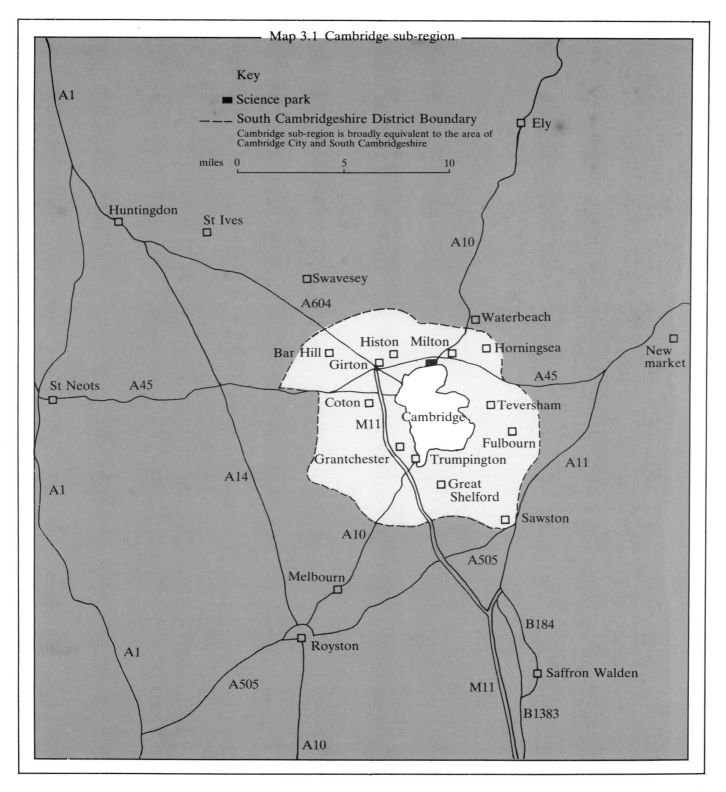

Map 3.1 Cambridge sub-region

Key

■ Science park

– – – South Cambridgeshire District Boundary
Cambridge sub-region is broadly equivalent to the area of
Cambridge City and South Cambridgeshire

miles 0   5   10

transfer, and the kinds of highly trained people concerned are typically readily mobile. There is undoubtedly an unusually high incidence of such movement in Cambridge. It has unfortunately been beyond our resources even to attempt to construct a tree showing the movement of all individuals into and out of local organisations.

3.24 The tree similarly does not purport to show three other types of links; financial, technological and trading. Again this is not because they are unimportant – the last two have been especially so in the past, and the first is becoming so – but because it was beyond the scope of this study to assemble such detailed material.

3.25 An exercise of this kind inevitably contains some anomalies and runs the risk of omissions or other errors. We sought to guard against this by cross-checking the preliminary information we had compiled on it with each company (whether as parent or child) and also getting comments on the whole chart from individuals with wide knowledge of local business developments. Nevertheless, some errors may remain and we apologise where they arise.

3.26 The family tree, apart from its intrinsic interest, helps illuminate the role of the University in respect of new company formation. Only a relatively small proportion (approximately 17%) of new company formation has been by individuals coming straight from the University (or still remaining in it). But the University has indirectly been the ultimate origin of virtually all of the other companies on the chart. This is because first generation spin-outs from the University have themselves spawned new companies and so on; also even where the 'parent' companies have not come from the University, the latter has constituted a basic reason for the organisation concerned to be located in Cambridge in the first instance.

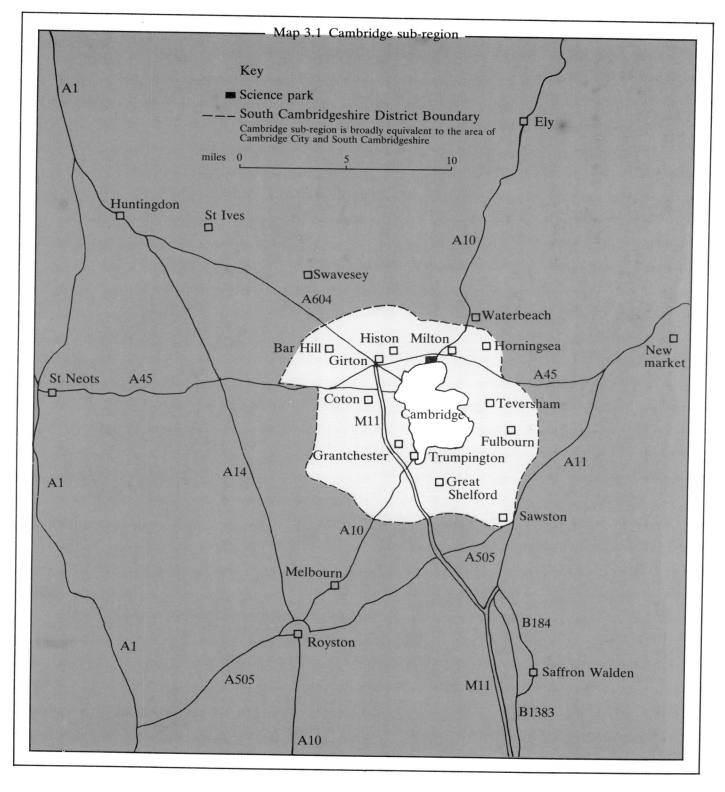

Map 3.1 Cambridge sub-region

Key

■ Science park

– – – South Cambridgeshire District Boundary

Cambridge sub-region is broadly equivalent to the area of Cambridge City and South Cambridgeshire

miles 0   5   10

A1

Ely

A10

Huntingdon

St Ives

Swavesey

A604

Waterbeach

Bar Hill

Histon

Milton

Horningsea

New market

Girton

St Neots

A45

A45

Coton

Teversham

M11

Cambridge

A1

A14

Fulbourn

Grantchester

Trumpington

A11

Great Shelford

A10

Sawston

A505

Melbourn

B184

A1

Royston

A505

Saffron Walden

M11

A10

B1383

transfer, and the kinds of highly trained people concerned are typically readily mobile. There is undoubtedly an unusually high incidence of such movement in Cambridge. It has unfortunately been beyond our resources even to attempt to construct a tree showing the movement of all individuals into and out of local organisations.

3.24 The tree similarly does not purport to show three other types of links; financial, technological and trading. Again this is not because they are unimportant – the last two have been especially so in the past, and the first is becoming so – but because it was beyond the scope of this study to assemble such detailed material.

3.25 An exercise of this kind inevitably contains some anomalies and runs the risk of omissions or other errors. We sought to guard against this by cross-checking the preliminary information we had compiled on it with each company (whether as parent or child) and also getting comments on the whole chart from individuals with wide knowledge of local business developments. Nevertheless, some errors may remain and we apologise where they arise.

3.26 The family tree, apart from its intrinsic interest, helps illuminate the role of the University in respect of new company formation. Only a relatively small proportion (approximately 17%) of new company formation has been by individuals coming straight from the University (or still remaining in it). But the University has indirectly been the ultimate origin of virtually all of the other companies on the chart. This is because first generation spin-outs from the University have themselves spawned new companies and so on; also even where the 'parent' companies have not come from the University, the latter has constituted a basic reason for the organisation concerned to be located in Cambridge in the first instance.

4

CAMBRIDGE HIGH TECHNOLOGY COMPANIES – 2: PATTERNS OF DEVELOPMENT AND OF INTERACTION WITH THE LOCAL ECONOMY

INTRODUCTION

4.1   The previous chapter presented a statistical outline of the Cambridge high technology company sector. Also the company family tree served to highlight the web of connections between many of the companies and to illuminate the indirect (even more than the direct) influence of the University in development of the sector.

4.2   The present chapter builds on this basic picture. In particular it discusses some of the salient features of the companies, paying special attention to the independent/indigenous* group. The chapter also notes the main recent developments on the local high technology scene, and concludes with some broad observations about Cambridge as a location for high technology activity compared with other developing centres of high technology in the UK.

CHARACTERISTICS OF THE FIRMS

Reasons for starting up and being in Cambridge

4.3   We asked the indigenous firms in the sample why they had started up in business. 'Pull' factors (perception of market opportunity, desire for independence, financial ambition, etc) were given as the dominant reason in just over two-thirds of the companies. 'Push' factors (frustration, lack of security in previous employment, uncertainty of research grant funding, etc) were dominant in a little under one quarter of the cases; they were particularly evident in the electrical equipment and instrument engineering sectors.

4.4   Interestingly, while we did not obtain systematic information on this point, not one response was in terms of there being a history of self-employment in their families. This factor has often been taken to be one of the most significant causes of a person's starting a business, but our strong impression is that it has been only a minor influence in Cambridge.

4.5   As to why the indigenous companies started up in the Cambridge area, by far the single most important answer (73% of the total) was that the principals lived there. This accords with the observation made in many other studies that at the time of start-up company

*Independent and indigenous are not exactly synonymous because some of the firms (only a few, but they are important ones) that began as both subsequently lost their independent status by being acquired by other firms. For simplicity for purposes of this discussion we include them in the 'indigenous' group.

founders seek to minimise their financial risks and physical inconvenience, and hence typically remain in their existing locality. In the Cambridge case, as will be discussed more fully later, there is the further question as to why there were so many company founders living in the Cambridge area to start with. In addition to local residence and continued contact with the University, there are reinforcing factors that are to do with existing local contacts and perception of local market opportunities as well as the prestigious address. Indeed, these last three factors were rated as the most important by those independent founders who did not cite local residence as the reason for a Cambridge start-up location.

4.6   Of the companies that moved into or set up in the area, in somewhat more than 75% of the cases the reasons for having a Cambridge location were to do with the presence of the University and other local research or high technology organisations and to the prestige of the address. This is as would be expected.

4.7   The combination of a local contact network, the presence of the University and increasingly of other high technology companies, and the Cambridge address has an implication of crucial importance to the companies: ease of recruitment of high calibre staff. Especially though not only amongst the technologically most advanced companies, the expectation and happily also the experience are that Cambridge is not only a good place in which to recruit but, of greater significance, also *to* which to recruit outstanding people.

Employment characteristics

4.8   A distinctive feature of the firms is, as one might expect, a high proportion of graduates on their payrolls. While about 25% of the sample reported no graduates, the rest averaged eight per company, and among all companies the mean proportion of graduates relative to total employment was one third. Across the sample as a whole Cambridge University accounted for 27% of all graduates, including those with both first and higher degrees.

4.9   We sought additional information on the composition of employment in the companies, recognising the inevitable difficulties in exact classification. In the population of firms as a whole staff in managerial (including financial, marketing and professional) occupations accounted for some 11% of total employment.

BOX 4.1 EICON RESEARCH LIMITED

Eicon Research is a young company, founded in 1979, that started 'soft' with the express commitment to 'harden' as soon as possible by way of producing leading edge hardware and software products typically on a customised basis. Despite its brief history and the fact that it is still quite small (some 30 staff and a turnover of around £3.5m) it exemplifies some of the critical elements in the 'hardening' process notably including the need for management and organisational development.

The founders were John Hartley who spun out of Cambridge Consultants (having previously worked at Tube Investment's research laboratories at Hinxton, and before that as a research student in the University engineering department), Tony Hooley who was on an IBM post-doctoral research fellowship in the physics department, and Beth Hutchison, also a doctorate in physics from the University, who left Applied Research of Cambridge to join the company full-time in 1982. The three, whose University research was all funded by the SERC, had met while students and had consciously kept in touch since they were each keen on starting a company.

Their start-up strategy was to undertake consultancy and contract R&D in electronics and computer software to finance product development; they also became sales agents for Apple and NEC. Wherever possible they sought to do only those R&D contracts on which they could keep the intellectual property rights and hence could potentially be converted into their own products. Their first product was a floppy disk sub-system for the Apple II, and currently their main product is a hard disk sub-system compatible with IBM, Apple and NEC equipment. The distinctive feature of their disk drive and their new networking products is their speed of operation, which is an order of magnitude faster than their competitors. Their perception of this market derived from their having been Apple agents.

Eicon is committed to continuing development of new products and its business thinking concentrates on product planning over at least a 2–3 year time horizon. Among its planned major new products are a workstation for a local CAD firm and a machine fatigue controller developed jointly with the University engineering department on SERC funding.

The company deliberately built a strong and balanced management team before seeking external finance and also before marketing in the USA (which now accounts for three-quarters of its business). It recruited experienced people from a number of international companies into the key marketing, production and financial positions, and launched its US effort by hiring the ex-editor of a leading US computer magazine. Among its most crucial appointments has been that of Dennis Taylor to chairman, on a free-ranging non-executive basis for two days a week; he was previously managing director of Hewlett Packard in the UK. As the scale and complexity of its operations have increased so has Eicon changed its professional advisors to those who, while still local, are more experienced in international business.

The company's structure remained informal until 1983, but with the growth in size and the emerging need for a strong marketing group this has now changed. The style is still informal, facilitated by a weekly meeting of the whole firm, but distinct functions and reporting responsibilities have been established.

Eicon has taken advantage of several government aid programmes. These have included the small firms loan guarantee scheme and the support for innovation scheme, the latter being crucial to one of their R&D projects. In 1984 the company, confident of its business strategy, negotiated external finance from a City of London institution in return for a minority equity stake.

Eicon finds Cambridge an outstanding business location. Apart from the founders' keeping up their personal links with the University, the company benefits by being able easily to recruit first-rate people who are willing to relocate to Cambridge if necessary because they know that there are a significant number of other interesting job opportunities in the area. A further advantage of Cambridge is the presence of a network of sub-contract companies who are able to produce very high quality, low volume work with minimal delays.

Qualified scientists and engineers were some 25% of the workforce. Putting these two categories together, and allowing for the overlap between them, we estimate that approximately one third of employment in all the high technology companies is in these higher grade skills; the corresponding proportion for companies established after 1974 is about 60% (of whom three quarters are qualified scientist and engineers). This is a remarkable rise in the technological/professional qualifications of the labour force, and is a reflection principally of the fact that many of these post-1974 start-ups have not yet grown and matured to a point where they employ a significant proportion of lower grade labour; it is also a reflection of the increasing need for advanced skills in high technology industry as well as the low incidence of production operations among the firms themselves.

4.10 This information points to the low proportion of 'ordinary' jobs among the newer firms, as would be expected. But because of high profits and high value added per employee, the firms generate above-average employment multiplier effects especially given the historically low wage levels in the local economy. The readily evident expansion and increasing sophistication of the retail, recreation and business and personal services sectors currently taking place must in good measure be due to the growth of local high technology industry; and these sectors mostly offer 'ordinary' employment.

4.11 We also sought to gauge the importance of employment problems as a constraint on the companies' development. Only one third reported serious problems in respect of their immediate development opportunities; the problem comprised shortages (in decreasing order of importance) of qualified scientists and engineers, technicians and skilled manual workers, and managerial staff. But as our face-to-face interviews made clear and almost as a truism, the limiting factor on the existing companies' long-term development, and on the formation of successful new companies, is high calibre people across a mix of managerial, business and technological skills. This is a complex question and will be returned to in a later chapter.

R&D and innovation
4.12 The sectors we concentrated on would generally be agreed to be high technology. Once we had established in each case that the firm's products/processes/services could reasonably be taken to be high tech-

nology, we asked two further questions:

(a) the percentage of R&D expenditure relative to turnover. This measure has been used in other studies but we found it rather unsatisfactory. Some firms did not identify R&D as a separate item in their accounts, and certain categories of firms (eg consultants and R&D contractors) could not properly distinguish in-house R&D from that done for clients. Nevertheless, the information obtained (for 189 companies) is revealing. Nearly two-thirds of companies reported an R&D/turnover ratio greater than 5%, and one in eight reported a ratio greater than 50%;

(b) the importance to the firm of technological development and innovation. Although an inexact question inviting a subjective answer, it too was revealing. More than 50% (of 260 firms responding) said "very important" and a further 20% "important". It was only in a few of the electronics goods sub-sectors that a small minority of firms said "very important".

4.13 These responses really did no more than confirm, and perhaps extend to a wider section of industry, what was already known about Cambridge high technology industry: viz there is a pronounced orientation towards research, design and development (as opposed to production and distribution). The nature and extent of this bias vary from one sector and one firm to another, but in all sectors there is a significant proportion of leading-edge activity.

Links with the local research complex
4.14 Links between the companies and the University and other local research institutions are clearly an item of some interest in this study. It is worth commenting, by way of introduction, that it is important to view such links, especially those of a very formal kind, in a wider perspective. Even leading edge companies do not necessarily need, and may not be able to cope with, formal relationships with research institutions. It is also important to recognise that the existence and nature of such links are a complex function of such factors as the age and size of firms, the relevant scientific disciplines and personal relationships. For instance, at the time of start-up, the most important source of technology for the indigenous companies is that embodied in key people (founders or other employees); this is supplemented over time, depending on the nature and growth of the firm, principally by in-house research, design and development and in a relatively minor way by sub-contracted research and consultancy.

BOX 4.2   SPECTRONICS MICRO SYSTEMS LIMITED

SMS represents an interesting example of a young company (established 1981) that started off at once with a 'hard' product range based on advanced technology both developed elsewhere by one of the founders and also bought in from a third source. One of these products has since provided the basis for the development of sophisticated mobile data communications systems.

The two founders were Roy Goss and Bev Ewen-Smith, finance and technical directors respectively of Laser-Scan, the scientific instruments company located on the Cambridge science park that had itself been spun-out from the Cavendish Laboratory in the late 1960s. Ewen-Smith, with a doctorate from the engineering department and a variety of employment experience, had been in charge of microprocessor applications in Laser-Scan. His work led into development of mobile data systems which, despite their recognised market potential, were felt by the parent company to lie outside their core business. Ewen-Smith and Goss, the latter providing the business expertise, decided to set up their own business to exploit this potential and accordingly bought the basic radio frequency signalling know-how and associated equipment from Laser-Scan along with LED display technology from a leading firm in this field based in York.

The LED systems quickly generated revenue by virtue of SMS's acquiring, along with the technology, a network of sales agents in Europe and the USA. On the radio frequency side the main customer was the Directorate of Telecommunications and the Ministry of Defence (Royal Signals and Radar Establishment) which had previously been a customer of Laser-Scan. The markets for both products have developed nicely and currently include major public and private sector clients in the UK and, more or less exclusively on the LED technology, a variety of clients on the Continent.

Exports are a little under 10% of total sales and the company recognises that they must be significantly further expanded and in particular the US market penetrated. Marketing and sales have recently been separated from production and made into a separate department though recruitment of a person of the requisite calibre is not proving easy and the services of a head-hunter are now being used. In addition, under a Department of Trade & Industry scheme, research has been commissioned into the market in the USA and elsewhere in order to formulate an effective marketing strategy.

SMS has recorded sound performance. In its first year, 1981/82, turnover was somewhat over £250 000 and this had approximately doubled by 1983/84. Employment rose from 10 to 24 over the same period; of the latter number, six were graduates (five from Cambridge, three recent engineering graduates).

Thus far the originally bought-in product technologies have remained central to the business. They have been further developed by in-house work (not formally organised) supplemented by a limited amount of consultancy placed with the University engineering department. The company maintains good informal links with the engineering department and uses the University library, though so far the main benefits of being located in Cambridge have been ease of recruitment of engineers, image especially for overseas marketing and ready access to precision sub-contractors based locally. Looking ahead, it sees significant marketing advantages accruing from the large number of small high technology companies in the locality and the openings afforded by growing inter-company contacts, and the ability to subcontract actual manufacture leaving them to concentrate on making best use of their advanced design expertise.

The company's original funding involved a combination of a term loan, backed by the government's loan guarantee scheme, overdraft facilities and investment by the founders. Little more than a year later it needed a further injection of capital and this was provided by a Scottish financial institution (its first investment in Cambridge) in return for a minority equity stake. Access to further finances, as and when necessary, is not considered a problem at this stage.

4.15 Given these comments it is striking that slightly over half of all the firms contacted maintained, or had done so in the past, links with the local research bodies. Most (90%) of these links were with University departments, these most frequently being engineering, physics and the computer laboratory. The linkages ranged, in broad terms, from sales of equipment (the least common) to informal contact (the most common). It is noteworthy too that for nearly 20% of the firms the links with the local research establishment provided a source of technology through collaborative projects, licensing or consultancy.

4.16 In addition, we suspect on the basis of our consultations and experience elsewhere that most companies, except those with the most obvious and major links, tend to understate their relationships with and (indirect) benefits from local research establishments; the relationships are diverse and complex, and certainly not gauged satisfactorily in the course of a telephone interview alone. Structured research projects are the exceptional kind of relationship; social contact, allowing for easy recruitment and 'picking of brains' by the companies as well as a demonstration effect back into the departments from the companies' evidently successful activities, is undoubtedly more common and of greater significance. It is perhaps for these reasons that a number of studies, including one on Cambridge science park companies (20), have tended to understate the number and significance of university-industry links in any given situation.

4.17 These considerations are reinforced by the small size and informal nature of Cambridge itself, as well as by the role of the University in constituting a direct source of company founders. We identified nearly 400 individuals who had played a primary role in formation of independent companies in the area; in a little over 15% of these cases the immediately previous employment (or place of study) had been in the local research establishments. With around 5% of employees of all the high technology companies being Cambridge graduates, it is easy to see how informal and easily unremarked but nevertheless productive links are kept up between the companies and the University.

Local sales and purchase links

4.18 Taken overall, the group of firms as a whole depend little on local input and output links: 74% and 72% respectively reported no or minor links of each

kind. This is not surprising; one would expect most high technology firms to have to operate in much wider market-places, though we were not able to assemble systematic quantitive information on sales and purchase for the sample as a whole.

4.19 Nevertheless, three fundamentally important points emerged from the in-depth company interviews and wider consultations. First, there is in the locality a network of small – very small, seldom more than three people – precision engineering businesses undertaking high quality, fast turn-round sub-contract work. Their presence is critical to the ability of the young and small high technology firms in computing and electronics hardware and in scientific instruments to compete effectively and to react quickly to changes in the market. We spoke to a few of the sub-contract firms, a good number of whom are spin-outs from the workshops of such organisations as the University laboratories and local instruments firms.

4.20 Second, the high degree of specialisation in the advanced technology market means that new market niches are continuously opening up in the local economy. This is especially important for some of the new software firms since it greatly facilitates their entry into business. The gaps are not confined to high technology suppliers alone; specialised opportunities arise for instance in software publications, for which Cambridge – by virtue of the long history of printing and publishing in the area – is fortuitously well suited. Some of the bigger local firms – eg Acorn Computers and Applied Research of Cambridge – play a vital role as primary contractors in generating these new market opportunities.

4.21 Third, because of the small size of the UK market, there is a powerful pressure on many of the high technology firms to engage in exports from relatively early on in their lives. The pressure to do so varies considerably among sectors and even more among individual firms – in contract R&D, for instance, we encountered some highly successful firms with no exports at all and others with exports at 20% of trade, and in computing software the ratio ranged from zero to 60%. In general, but with a few notable exceptions, the tendency has been to view the USA as the principal export market, though there are recent signs of increasing interest in Europe and the Far East.

BOX 4.3   SHAPE DATA LIMITED

Shape Data provides a particularly interesting example of formation and growth of a leading edge technology company on two counts. First, as a direct University spin-out its core technology has been based on expertise developed in the course of a substantial government-funded research programme in computer aided design. Second, its future has been secured as the R&D-based subsidiary of one of the major computer graphics organisations in the USA.

The company was founded in 1974 by four leading members of the computer aided design group at the computer laboratory in the University, who themselves put up the modest amounts of start-up capital required. Charles Lang (whose brother Jack was a founder of Topexpress) had taken an engineering degree at Cambridge and moved to MIT before being recruited back to establish the CAD group in 1965. He is widely regarded as having made a major contribution to Cambridge's becoming one of the world's leading CAD centres. Of the other founders Alan Grayer and Ian Braid had completed doctorates in the computer laboratory, while Peter Veenman had taken an engineering masters degree in Holland before joining the CAD group.

This group had developed a world technological lead in geometric modelling techniques over a 10-year period, funded by what was then the Science Research Council, and had also played a significant role in the early development of the CADCentre. Their particular expertise, combined with uncertainty about continued funding and a positive attitude from the head of department to their moving on to other things, led to the establishment of Shape Data as a commercial CAD consultancy.

Peter Veenman was the first to work full-time in the company, which was initially given 'sheltered' accommodation and office facilities by Applied Research of Cambridge. He was followed 18 months later by another founder with the other two joining full-time in 1978 and 1980 respectively. Their consultancy put them in touch with a major UK electronics company in the defence field for whom they developed the first version of their geometry modelling CAD system. They continued consultancy to fund further development of the so-called Romulus system which was originally launched in 1978 and has since provided the main basis of the company's success. Sold on an OEM basis to large engineering companies

and other CAD-CAM firms, Romulus provides a complete system for modelling 3-dimensional shapes in the mechanical engineering industry. It is an especially advanced system, ahead of 'standard' CAD technology that is widely accepted, and consequently the clients themselves are typically highly sophisticated technologically.

The company remained technology driven as it grew from 10 to over 60 employees between 1974 and 1984.

By 1981 it became clear that to fund the scale of R&D effort needed to ensure its technological lead the firm required access to greater financial resources; up until then it had been self-financing. It also recognised that its management and particular marketing resources needed strengthening. After turning down the approaches of a major UK company whose style they felt did not match their own, the founders sold out to Evans & Sutherland of Salt Lake City, Utah. An informal relationship between the principals in both companies had existed for some years since there had been close contact between the CAD group at the Cambridge computer laboratory and the University of Utah, which was the major centre for computer graphics in the USA. Moreover, in 1979 Evans & Sutherland (who as individuals had their origins in the University of Utah) had become sales agents for Shape Data in the USA.

Evans & Sutherland have provided financial and management resources combined with marketing and sales expertise which have allowed Shape Data to concentrate on development of new CAD systems and maintain its technological lead. Evans & Sutherland also manufacture the hardware needed to drive the specialist software. Currently some 60% of Shape Data's business is overseas, with sales now handled by the parent firm.

Despite its origins, Shape Data no longer maintains formal links with the University. Since some 20 Cambridge graduates – many with PhD experience – work in the firm, however, there are numerous informal links particularly with the computer laboratory. A central Cambridge location is important to the firm; in addition to benefiting from the prestige it confers, it also allows the maintenance of close informal contact with other leading edge companies. This is an important factor in Shape Data's remaining a highly innovative CAD firm.

Financial aspects

4.22 All the evidence we have assembled from the companies themselves and the concerned business community points to what is an unusual conclusion for Britain: taken in aggregate and with seemingly few individual exceptions, the availability of finance has not been a limiting factor on formation and growth of the Cambridge high technology firms. This is all the more remarkable when one considers the frankly esoteric nature of the technologies and markets in many cases and hence, one might expect, an extra degree of nervousness of outside investors to back the projects.

4.23 Three main factors underly this conclusion. First, the start-up circumstances and strategy of many of the companies were such as to minimise their need for external finance until they were rather better established and 'bankable'. (These points are elaborated in chapter 6.)

4.24 Second, as already noted, from 1978 on an ad hoc basis and from 1980 more systematically the local regional office of Barclays Bank (which already had the accounts of a number of young high technology companies) took the decision to be as supportive as possible to new such ventures in the future. In financial terms, this was done either by means of an overdraft facility or a term loan, in some cases using the Bank's own special start-up scheme and where appropriate using the government's loan guarantee scheme for small firms. In the early 1980s Barclays came to dominate lending activity to new technology ventures in the area. The overall result was a ready availability of debt finance for start-up and early development purposes, to supplement the young firms' own resources.

4.25 The supportive role played by Barclays went significantly further than provision of finance alone. Very substantial inputs of management time were expressly committed to helping the high technology entrepreneurs prepare their business plans and set up their businesses, as well as to monitor and advise them through their early growth; such commitment and involvement by a clearing bank must stand as exceptional so far in Britain, whether in high technology or otherwise. In addition, Barclays helped the young entrepreneurs in other practical ways – for example introducing them to professional advisors in the local business community and providing the secretariat for the Cambridge Computer Group (see chapter 5).

4.26 Third, building on the early financing role being played by Barclays and other bodies such as the National Research Development Corporation and the Industrial and Commercial Finance Corporation, new sources of investment capital increasingly entered the market (and continue to do so now). Much of this money was limited to second- or later-round financing, but some was used for new starts too. The availability of this finance reflected in part the growth of the UK venture capital industry, and the activity in Cambridge of those few funds in the industry willing to become substantially involved in high technology and young projects. It reflected also the small but growing financial interest that a few of the Cambridge colleges were taking in the phenomenon, the appearance in the local scene of investment trusts and individuals looking for deals, and the increasing ability and willingness of successful Cambridge high technology companies themselves to make equity investments in new business ventures.

4.27 In addition to these Cambridge-specific factors, from the late 1970s onwards there became available across the country as a whole an increasing number of government schemes both for promoting innovation and also (but separately) small firms.

4.28 Taking the small firms measures first, the incentive of greatest interest is the scheme under which, for small business projects of an agreed kind, central government guarantees a proportion of the loan advanced by a clearing bank. This proportion was originally 80% but in mid-1984 was reduced to 70%. Our enquiries of the firms themselves identified 25 that had been financed under this arrangement. This is certainly an under-estimate for our (not fully comprehensive) enquiries of the clearing banks suggested a figure nearer 30, all for start-up purposes. Using this latter figure, this represents over 50% of the independent firms in our data bank that started up after June 1981 when the scheme came into operation. We do not have the evidence to add to the debate on the overall cost-effectiveness of the loan guarantee scheme and on the distribution of the risk among the parties concerned; but we can confirm the views of local bank managers that the scheme has contributed to the readier availability of term debt finance to the young companies in Cambridge.

4.29 The business expansion scheme is the second device the government has adopted to facilitate the financing of small firms. We came across its use only in three instances, one for a new start. There is little expectation locally that this scheme will play a significant role in the future, though it may become more used in funding of larger-scale expansion projects.

4.30 Central government operates a large number of measures in a 'support for innovation' package (SFI). DTI records show a rate of application for and utilisation of such support among Cambridgeshire firms well above the national average. Our own enquiries of high technology firms only suggest that about 20% of them have made successful applications for SFI.

4.31 The various elements of the SFI package differ too much in their applicability and rules for our telephone enquiries to reveal special insights into each of them individually. But we were struck both by the warm endorsements of them by some companies, and by the criticisms by others that applications took too long to be processed to be useful, especially in relation to what were very short product development periods, and that the schemes tended to be unsuited to start-up and very young firms.

4.32 Statistical analysis of our survey results showed clearly that the larger and better established firms – though mostly still small firms – were the more frequent users of SFI. For instance, of the firms reporting SFI use only 7% had fewer than five employees while 40% had above 30 employees. Similarly, the majority of users had turnover of £1 million or more. Analysis by age shows that only 20% of users had been established since 1980. These findings are not surprising; start-up and very young companies seldom have the capacity to handle highly specific grant applications, and it is only as they become more experienced in such matters and have greater management resources that they can more readily do so.

4.33 We do not have the evidence to comment authoritatively on the cost-effectiveness or otherwise of the SFI package. The schemes have undoubtedly been helpful in those cases where they have been taken up and have been one of the elements in achieving the situation where lack of finance has generally not been a constraint on development of the high technology sector in Cambridge.

Premises

4.34 In those cases (195 companies) where we secured satisfactory information 50% were housed in modern (sometimes purpose-built) light industrial cum office premises, nearly 25% in offices, 15% in specially converted buildings and 10% in ordinary industrial buildings. Tenure was leasehold in 70% of these cases, freehold in 30%.

4.35 It has sometimes been said that shortage of premises, both absolutely and in terms of suitability, has been a constraint on Cambridge's industrial development. But we found no real evidence of this: fully 80% of the firms consulted reported no serious past or current problems with premises. (Of the remaining 20%, half said that they then needed more space, one quarter said that their premises were not entirely suitable for their particular purposes and one quarter complained of planning problems.) This situation is perhaps not surprising; since the firms were small their premises needs were small too, and it was possible for them to be accommodated more easily into what happened to be available.

4.36 Nevertheless there is a host of local stories about the 'hassles' individual firms have had to go through in getting the premises they wanted, or in having to operate from more than one site. This stems in part from the desire, at least up to around 1980, of many of the young companies to be in or very near the city centre where virtually by definition accommodation is very tight; in part from the fact that at the start-up and formative phases small firms want to spend as little as possible on property and are prepared to improvise (and have been able to do so successfully); and in part also from the relatively modest supply until recently of better quality property suited to fast growing (though still small) firms whose success makes them increasingly image-conscious. But none of these problems seems so far to have seriously inhibited the firms' development, and we know of no cases where start-up has been prevented by lack of premises. The planners and the firms themselves have shown great skill in achieving this in an area which has not 'inherited' much by way of surplus industrial and commercial property and in which there have been few new developments of any scale.

4.37 The Cambridge science park (see box 4.4 for explanation of its origins) marks the first new develop-

BOX 4.4 CAMBRIDGE SCIENCE PARK

To many people in Britain (some even in Cambridge itself) and abroad, Cambridge high-technology industry and the Cambridge science park (CSP) are virtually synonymous. As this study amply shows this is far from being the actual case: in terms simply of the numbers of companies, for instance, CSP accounts for a small proportion (a little over 10%) of the overall high technology scene. And yet, also as demonstrated, the science park has steadily grown in importance, and it is no accident that it has become a prestigious symbol of Cambridge success in advanced technology.

The decision to establish the science park was taken in 1970 by Trinity College which owned the land. In 1969 the Mott report had articulated the growing conviction in the University that it was imperative to the long-term vitality of Cambridge research in the physical and natural sciences that science-based industry should be attracted to the area. Central government too was expressing concern about the national need for closer academic-industrial liaison. A further vital and very practical reason for the decision to proceed was the availability of a suitable site: a 130-acre block of land on the north-eastern edge of the city, that had remained unused for over 20 years and was expensive to restore to agricultural purposes as much of it had been a tank marshalling yard in the second world war.

That the land belonged to Trinity College was particularly fortunate. For Trinity, a substantial property investor, possessed the financial resources and the experience to drive the scheme through and could also afford to take a long view of its role and financial performance. Trinity has, too, from Isaac Newton onwards a roll-call of distinguished scientists that is unsurpassed; it has had more Nobel laureates than many countries, including for instance France. Moreover in the college's senior bursar, Dr John Bradfield – a life-long Cambridge man, a zoologist who had worked in the Cavendish before developing his commercial and administrative career – there was somebody who not only knew his way round the University administration and scientific community but who also understood the property development industry in all its aspects. The fact that Dr Bradfield and the locally based property management and letting agents Bidwells have remained responsible for the scheme from the outset has brought continuity and a capacity to learn from practical experience that have proved invaluable to orderly and quality development of the scheme.

The benefits of an unhurried long-term approach, working informally and in line with the natural grain of events, that is characteristic of much of Cambridge are also clearly evident in the matter of university-industry links. There is no elaborate or specially created mechanism to cultivate these links, which after modest beginnings have become an increasingly significant feature in the past few years. Dr Bradfield has made it his business gently to seek to get to know the tenants and broadly to understand their problems and needs; and then through his network of connections into all disciplines in the University (and the outside financial community if necessary) to ensure that the companies and the relevant experts meet each other informally and thus have the opportunity, if mutually interested, to establish working links. It is perhaps a 'laid-back' approach compared with arrangements elsewhere, but it is realistic and it is working.

Trinity's commitment to fostering academic-industry links has been underlined by its scheme to pay up to half the annual costs for 2–3 researchers who will divide their time roughly equally between their employers at the park and the University laboratories. The scheme, with initial total funding of £60 000 for three years, commenced in 1983 and was extended in 1984 with an additional £300 000 to be spent over six years.

The Trinity Centre – providing common room, bar and meeting rooms – was opened in 1984 as the College's latest contribution towards encouraging contact between tenant companies.

Trinity's aims for the science park have steadily evolved as the development has matured. The current aims may be summarised as follows:

(a) to provide a pleasant environment where high technology units ranging from 800 sq ft to over 100 000 sq ft can be rapidly and easily provided in order to encourage and facilitate development of such industry in Cambridge;

(b) to provide abundant and varied contact between the companies at the CSP and University departments (personal introductions, advertisement of University functions and seminars, joint research schemes, etc);

(c) encouragement of abundant and varied contacts between CSP companies themselves (twice annual newsletter, register of specialised equipment offered by CSP companies for shared use, Trinity Centre, etc).

ment of scale and quality and since the early 1980s has come to play a profoundly important role in the overall phenomenon. The park has attracted a great deal of national and international interest (eg see reference 7), and it will be useful to discuss its development more fully.

4.38 Because of the favourable climate engendered by the Mott committee, a liberal planning permission was eventually granted by the county council to the park, which stands in its principles and actual application as an excellent model of its kind throughout the country. This, in brief summary, has confined use of the park to:

(a) scientific research associated with industrial production;

(b) light industrial production dependent on consultation with the tenant's own research staff or with the local scientific establishment;

(c) ancillary activities considered appropriate to a science park (eg social centre, patent agents, venture capitalists).

4.39 The park has been developed in phases. The first two phases (56 acres) have now been completed, the third phase (26 acres) is mostly complete and the fourth phase (26 acres) is now getting under way.

4.40 The first tenant – Laser-Scan, a spin-out from the Cavendish that had been temporarily housed in the University – moved in in September 1973. Lettings proceeded quite slowly for the first five years: by 1978 there were only seven tenants on the first phase of 28 acres. But since the turn of the decade the rate of occupation has been faster, partly because of the growth in the number of high technology companies in the area and partly because of the provision of nursery units for start-up and very small companies. By mid-1984 there was a total of nearly 40 tenants, occupying some 370 000 square feet and providing employment for a little over 1 000 people. The popularity of the science park has evidently not been diminished by its having much the highest rents for industrial-style space in the area.

4.41 Trinity College itself has undertaken the majority of the infrastructure investment and has acted as developer/financier of most of the premises which are leased to tenants on terms agreed before construction (except for a few nursery units developed speculatively to obtain economy of scale). A recently opened social

centre for tenant companies has also been financed by the college, with outside support for purchasing furniture and equipment. Six companies, taking long leases on the land, have custom-built their premises at their own expense; they include the Industrial Commercial and Finance Corporation whose East Anglian regional office has recently relocated from elsewhere in Cambridge to the park and which has also put up 17 nursery units; these were let in advance except for a couple which were intended for start-ups.

4.42 A great deal of attention has been paid to landscaping, involving generous provision of trees and open water and construction of mounds. The ratio of buildings to land is low, approximately 1 : 6 which may be compared with a ratio of perhaps 1 : 2 on a conventional industrial estate. The quality of the development, along with its scale and its excellent siting in relation to the road system (A45 east–west and M11/A604/A1 north–south), has made CSP undoubtedly the most attractive location available so far in the Cambridge area for large international companies to establish their mobile projects or their 'listening posts' to detect what is going on in the local research laboratories.

4.43 The success of CSP and the readily evident buoyancy of demand have encouraged a number of new, quality developments to get under way. These, all undertaken by the private sector and mostly in Cambridge itself, are currently in varying stages of implementation. St John's College is proposing a science park on land directly opposite Trinity's development; a prestige development is now under construction for small high technology firms on a site next to (and available on long lease from) the county council, just outside but 10 minutes walk away from the city centre; other schemes and proposals, some quite large, are in the pipeline; at Melbourn a little further away from Cambridge but very much part of the phenomenon, there is a highly successful scheme for small high technology firms based on conversion of the premises formerly occupied by Metals Research.

4.44 The experience of Cambridge in the high technology property sector stands in interesting contrast to approaches being adopted elsewhere where high technology industry is being deliberately encouraged, on three main counts. First, in Cambridge the provision of property has by and large followed rather than been ahead of demand – in most other areas property is

BOX 4.5 SINCLAIR RESEARCH LIMITED

Sinclair Research occupies a prominent position in Cambridge by virtue of several special factors: the career of Clive Sinclair himself, the high turnover and rapid growth of the company, its distinctive approach to the organisation of production, and the factors that led to its location in Cambridge.

Sinclair's early career was spent as a technical journalist in north London. But his real interest lay in audio and electronic inventions and while trying to find a way to start his own business he met in 1961 Tim Eiloart, who had founded Cambridge Consultants the previous year. Sinclair Radionics was established in London in 1962; its first products were radio and amplifier kits sold by mail order from Cambridge with the assistance of Cambridge Consultants. Sinclair kept in touch with the Cambridge scene and in 1967 relocated his expanding business, then also making hi-fi systems, to Cambridge and in 1972 to St Ives.

Sinclair's particular interest and pioneering skill lay in the miniaturisation of consumer electronic goods. He is credited with having produced the world's first truly pocket calculator in 1972; by 1973 the company dominated the UK calculator market. There followed a period of heavy investment in R&D into a range of new products, notably including digital watches and a pocket TV. Design and component supply difficulties for the watches drained the company's resources after 15 years of growth, and in 1976 the newly founded National Enterprise Board invested in the company to ensure realisation of the TV project.

In 1979, although the pocket TV and a variety of other new products had been successfully produced, the NEB saw the future of the company as lying in the instrument field whereas Sinclair saw it in consumer electronics. The solution was to divide the company's interests: the NEB retained the instruments business (subsequently relaunched as Thandar Electronics) and Sinclair established Sinclair Research in Cambridge in 1979 in the consumer electronics market. A number of other new enterprises were established in the area at the time of the break-up of Sinclair Radionics.

The aim of Sinclair Research, 85% owned by Sinclair himself, is to research, develop and market advanced consumer electronics products. The initial focus was on the home computer market, but this has now broadened to include business and educational computers and flat-screen pocket televisions.

Concentration on highly competitive consumer markets has had the effect of transforming the company from previously being technology-driven to being market-pulled, although still highly technologically innovative. Hence while the products were initially sold by mail order, as the volume of sales has grown so it has become important to get fast feedback from the market directly

into new design and development. Consequently Sinclair Research has become more directly concerned in establishing effective channels of distribution. In the UK it uses several thousand retail outlets, though overseas it operates through its own subsidiaries. Expansion into overseas markets – including recent penetration into China – has been a prominent feature of its efforts, and exports account for around 60% of business.

Sinclair Research sub-contracts all its volume production and also as much of its prototype or other specialist supplies as possible. This policy, derived directly from the experience of Sinclair Radionics, enables the company to concentrate its resources on research, design and development which is where its special skills lie. The large-scale subcontract work is done in London, Scotland and in the future also in Korea; but some work is placed with local Cambridge electronics hardware firms and also software specialists and technical writers.

Another feature of the company is the policy of recruiting, internationally if necessary, only the very best individuals for senior management and key technological positions. Interestingly most of the directors, including Nigel Searle (the managing director – Sinclair himself is executive chairman), have been associated with Sinclair since the 1960s.

Growth of turnover of Sinclair Research has been spectacular by UK standards: five years after start-up it is of the order of £80m. Because of the no-production policy total direct employment is only about 100, most of it in Cambridge. There are only six Cambridge graduates among the employees.

The company's headquarters and main activities are on two sites in Cambridge, both high quality refurbishments/extensions of nineteenth-century buildings. One of these houses the new Metalab, the group responsible for long-range product development. There are also smaller groups in London, Winchester and Boston, Mass. (Sinclair Vehicles, an independent company owned wholly by Sinclair himself, which carries out R&D into an advanced electric car, is based in Warwick.)

Cambridge remains an invaluable location for Sinclair, despite the absence of formal or close connections with the University. The benefits to the company have been ease of quality recruitment (especially in the early years), an informal social network of like-minded and forward-looking technologists, and a prestigious address.

There have been benefits to Cambridge too. The singular career and success of Sinclair have conferred prestige on Cambridge as a high technology location. And Sinclair, along with a few others, has become a role model for the young local companies because of his financial success and also his approach to the organisation of production.

being used as an instrument to stimulate demand. Second, the private sector has dominated provision in Cambridge (and continues to do so), where elsewhere it is the public sector. And third, until quite recently, Cambridge property has generally been quite conventional with few if any special features in the buildings themselves – elsewhere there is a tendency to believe that high technology firms, even those at start-up or in very early stages of development, necessarily require premises that are themselves high technology in some way.

Business services

4.45 As a prosperous market and university town in a thriving agricultural area, Cambridge has long been well endowed with local firms in business and professional services and has also had good connections with large firms in London. Building on this traditional pattern, and in response to the burgeoning high technology sector, a variety of new developments have taken place over the past decade and at a quickening pace more recently.

4.46 First, some of the long-established firms have developed new departments and specialised capabilities to service the high technology firms. A good example of this is one of the largest legal practices setting up a commercial department in the early 1970s expressly for this purpose.

4.47 Second, individuals already in the area have set up their own new firms to supply specialist services. Among the best known cases, also dating from the first half of the 1970s, are a firm of patent agents (Keith W Nash & Co whose founder spun out from Metals Research) and a firm offering high-level recruitment services (Cambridge Recruitment Consultants which spun out of Sinclair Radionics), both of which now operate internationally. More recently, several other firms have been set up offering financial, business consulting and venture management services.

4.48 Third, the last few years have seen the arrival in Cambridge of several of the major national/international firms of accountants/management consultants and property agents. A City of London merchant bank will be opening an office in Cambridge shortly, and similarly a major law firm is said to be considering doing so.

4.49 Fourth, a still small but growing number of individuals of substantial business experience are entering the Cambridge scene. Their role is to supply financial, marketing, negotiating and general management skills to complement the skills of the technological entrepreneurs. Some individuals may divide their time among more than one high technology firm. People offering this kind of service have been active in Cambridge for some while, and perhaps inevitably their performance has sometimes been regarded as unsatisfactory and has not been without controversy. What seems to be new, however, is that the increasing success and sophistication of the Cambridge phenomenon has come to attract individuals of high calibre and international experience into the local business network.

Physical communications

4.50 The substantial improvements to the strategic road system serving Cambridge that have taken place in the past 5–10 years have already been noted. The companies feel that their immediate impact has been three-fold:

(a) to increase the accessibility of Cambridge to most parts of the country, London and the east coast port of Felixstowe being probably the most valuable connections. Within the next year it will be only to the south and west Midlands areas that road connections will be poor;

(b) to open up the Cambridge hinterland, especially to the west and northwest, for commuting;

(c) to facilitate the integration of Huntingdon/St Ives and Melbourn, with which there were already good business and other links, into the wider Cambridge business (especially high technology) scene.

4.51 The improved road system has had a psychological benefit too, to the companies as well as more generally. Cambridge now no longer 'feels' remote; of particular consequence, London and Cambridge now seem very close. The planned upgrading of the rail service between the two cities will reinforce these perceptions.

4.52 Cambridge's principal strategic transport deficiency is with respect to airport access. Heathrow and Gatwick are around two hours' distance by car, though the time to the former will be reduced (and the journey made much easier) when the M25 link connecting the M11 and M4 is completed. Stansted is only a 30-minute car drive away but its services are limited though improving. If Stansted were to be declared the third London airport, the potential impact on Cambridge would be enormous – this issue is noted again briefly in chapter 8.

Cambridge as a business location

4.53 The picture that emerges from this and the previous chapter is that over say the past three decades Cambridge has come a long way from being a fine university and market town with a concentration of scientific capability and a sprinkling of science-based enterprises. Many elements – technology, commercial, physical, policy – have come together in such a way as to have begun to build up a substantial business community in the area. Perhaps surprisingly to those who think of it in a traditional sense, these and other factors (which will be discussed in the next chapter) have also contributed towards making Cambridge an excellent location for small high technology businesses in particular.

4.54 All our consultations, both with the firms themselves and others, confirmed this view. Remarkably few adverse comments were made; even the well-known car parking and congestion problems in the city centre attracted only moderate criticism. In any event the trend, noted above, for new industrial/commercial property development to be located on the periphery of the city centre or on the outskirts of the city should ease these problems in the future.

THE ROLE OF CAMBRIDGE IN THE DEVELOPMENT OF UK HIGH TECHNOLOGY INDUSTRY

4.55 It is evident from the foregoing that, with certain obvious exceptions, the typical Cambridge high technology firm is young, small, indigenous and independent, and does not undertake production in-house but is rather engaged in activities with a high research, design and development content. As the phenomenon matures, so this pattern is changing and new kinds of firm will become established in the area – this is discussed in chapter 8. Nevertheless, it is instructive to contrast Cambridge as it has evolved to date with two other areas of the country in which there are concentrations of high technology industry: central Scotland and the M4 corridor running west from London to Bristol.

4.56 Up to now electronics has been by far the most important high technology industry in Scotland. It has been dominated by subsidiary operations undertaken by large, mostly US multinational companies over the past 30 years. The first generation of sizeable inward investment was in the 1950s and 1960s in production of electro-mechanical systems, made by such US companies as IBM, Burroughs, Honeywell, NCR and Hewlett Packard; they were attracted in part by the existing technology base built up after the second world war around the defence electronics work undertaken by two major UK firms, Ferranti and Marconi. As these major plants have switched into new, wholly electronic systems, so there has been a second wave of foreign investment in the central belt of the country; a succession of major US and Japanese semiconductor producers have invested in production of specialised microelectronic components and products. The consequence is that Scotland has developed a very large electronics industry, comprising nearly 300 companies and more than 40 000 employees, located mainly in a broad belt across the centre of the country.

4.57 The foreign investment projects are typically very large. In integrated circuits, for instance, the large companies' plants account for over 20% of European output. A further interesting feature is that while they have usually started as production only they have tended in addition to develop more sophisticated technological and also marketing functions. In parallel with this latter trend has been the development of an indigenous Scottish sector: establishment of new small firms spinning out from the big companies and from the universities, engaged in such sectors as medical instrumentation, data processing systems, sub-contract services and software design and consultancy. Indigenous ventures – which numbered perhaps eight a year in the early 1980s – are probably increasing now, given the efforts of the Scottish Development Agency and an increasingly active private financial sector. Even so they form a small part of the total picture: in 1983 indigenous companies accounted for about one sixth of employment in the Scottish electronics industry (10). But there is evidence of a well developed technological capability in these local companies (24), and there is a general confidence that the indigenous electronics sector will perform strongly in future years.

4.58 The pattern of involvement of Scottish universities in development of high technology industry has also been quite different from that of Cambridge. It is true that they have been important as sources of

---

BOX 4.6 TOPEXPRESS LIMITED

Topexpress is an excellent example of a company with strong roots in and continuing links with the University. It depends on ready access to graduates and research workers of outstanding capability, and on the free exchange of ideas with University staff; five of its own staff hold college fellowships. For these reasons the company's various premises are in the centre of the city.

The company was formed in 1978 by John Ffowcs-Williams (professor of acoustics in the engineering department, who combines academic duties with part-time work for the firm), and Jack Lang (a Cambridge graduate who had previously been a demonstrator in computer science in the University computing laboratory). Immediately prior to establishing Topexpress both principals had had brief involvement in a new business with a third person whose particular role was to handle the commercial and marketing aspects to complement their own technological expertise. When this earlier relationship proved unsatisfactory, they decided to establish a new company themselves and were able to carry a number of accounts with them. Their original motivation to engage in business arose from their increasing volume of external consultancy work which they were undertaking as dons, and in Lang's case also from a recognition that in an academic career he would have to wait longer than he would like to have a substantial management responsibility.

Topexpress has rapidly become one of the country's leading scientific and software consultancies. Its contracts are typically of long duration, involving the development of mathematical models and specialist software for solving fundamental problems of government and industry.

Its main clients are in the UK (notably including the Ministry of Defence, and Acorn Computers), and as the reputation of the company grows so new clients are being established abroad particularly in the US.

At start-up there were the two founders plus a programmer and an administrative assistant. In early 1984 there were some 40 staff, of whom all except secretaries and cleaning employees were graduates, and over 20 staff had higher degrees. Turnover has risen more than twenty-fold in the same period, from some £50 000 in the first year.

Topexpress has remained a 'soft' company, to use the jargon of this report. It did attempt to go 'hard' on one particular product but withdrew when it became evident that it did not readily have the requisite marketing skills. Interestingly, one of the companies spinning-out from Topexpress did so specifically to produce a 'hard' product.

Topexpress's success and growth have been achieved without sacrificing the informal style that characterises young and very small 'boffin' companies. The basic management unit is the particular team assembled for each project, and because of the relaxed style of the company, the intense interest of each assignment and an employee profit-sharing scheme there is no difficulty in motivating staff.

---

graduate recruitment – this is one of the reasons for a project being undertaken by Wang near Stirling University; in certain sectors they are at the leading edge of research (such as in artificial intelligence at Edinburgh University, opto-electronics at Glasgow and Heriot-Watt, and medical physics at Aberdeen); and there is everywhere a rising incidence of university-industry research collaboration. But up to the present at least they have not been sources of new technology ventures in any numbers.

4.59 The pattern of development of the M4 corridor is equally distinctive. Despite the absence of regional financial aid – though with special, local marketing efforts notably by Swindon and Bristol – this area has proved very attractive to high technology industry. Data provided by the Department of Trade & Industry showed that in April 1984 there were nearly 150 establishments (in the size range above 10 employees, with aggregate employment among them of some 20 000) in Berkshire, Wiltshire and Avon, in the instru-ment engineering, telecommunications and electronics manufacturing industries. Twenty of the plants were foreign-owned; but of the 17 plants that had opened since 1976 only one was foreign. The principal activities undertaken in these establishments are marketing, distribution and production (mostly assembly), with a certain amount of R&D. In addition to these industries, the UK computer services industry is heavily concentrated in the South East region, mostly in the London area but with a strong presence west of London in the Reading area (9b); and the advanced biotechnology industry is also well represented in and around Slough.

4.60 A variety of factors explain this spatial pattern (3, 9a): a general trend to location outside London and in smaller and more congenial environments, for cost and 'lifestyle' reasons; excellent road and rail communications to London, and national and international air communications through Heathrow; the building-up of a large pool of highly specialised labour (for instance in applications software in the Reading–Bracknell area); and a certain amount of spin-out of independent new companies from existing larger establishments though the latter (which are mostly subsidiaries of companies based elsewhere) are still dominant. The presence of a university or research establishment is widely thought not to have been a material factor in development of the M4 high technology sector; though once established a company may form such links as is happening at Hewlett Packard's European R&D centre being established in Bristol (near one of its existing assembly plants) where links are being cultivated particularly with the adjacent polytechnic.

4.61 It is evident that all three areas discussed have become successfully established in high technology activity via quite different routes: Scotland mainly by attraction of mobile, large production projects from abroad; the M4 corridor through a combination of 'spontaneous' industrial movement and the attractions of a highly accessible, high quality environment; and Cambridge through indigenous growth associated with the presence of the University, as we saw. Each area is becoming a little less specialised as it develops. For instance, Scotland and the M4 are undergoing some backwards vertical integration (distribution leads to production, which leads to R&D, and so on) and the frequency of new enterprise formation is probably rising, in the case particularly of Scotland based on the strong research capabilities in the local universities. The significant new trend in Cambridge's growth is the arrival of companies from outside, and there is as yet only mild pressure for vertical integration forwards into volume production – these points are discussed again in chapter 8.

4.62 The scale of development in Cambridge is much smaller in absolute terms than in the other two locations. But of course there is a great disparity in the populations of the respective labour catchment areas: less than a quarter of a million in the case of Cambridge as against several millions in the other two cases. In relative terms, however, there appears to be little difference among them: indeed, Cambridge and Scotland seem to have about the same proportion (around one sixth) of total employment in high technology industry.

4.63 All in all, therefore, Cambridge stands up very well in comparison with the other main areas of high technology growth in the UK. And given that the phenomenon has been 'driven' essentially by indigenous, independent small companies – most of which have started up over the past decade, a period of almost unabated economic recession in Britain – it seems fair to conclude that it (the phenomenon) is of national not just local consequence.

COMPARISONS WITH OTHER HIGH TECHNOLOGY AREAS

4.64 How does Cambridge compare with other centres of high technology industry? Special research would be needed to answer this question satisfactorily, because of the formidable methodological difficulties of any such comparison and the lack of equivalent data among the locations of relevance.

4.65 But the question is worth pursuing a little – especially in relation to Silicon Valley in California and Route 128 in Boston – for two main reasons. First, because of its intrinsic interest. Second, because it helps illuminate something that will become increasingly evident as the Cambridge story unfolds in later chapters, viz there is a multiplicity of factors causing and shaping not just the rate of growth and the overall scale of high technology industry in any one location, but also the particular forms that such growth and the industry itself take.

4.66 To take first the matter of the point in time at which the comparison might be made. A recent estimate (30) puts the number of high technology firms in Silicon Valley at a little over 1 200, employing around 190 000 (with nearly another 1 000 firms elsewhere in the San Francisco Bay area, accounting for a further 40 000 jobs). In the numbers of businesses and employees, as well as in average employees per firm, these figures represent a scale of development several orders of magnitude larger than Cambridge as presented earlier in the chapter.

4.67 But of course it is a false comparison, insofar as the high technology sector in Santa Clara county (Silicon Valley) started to 'explode' in the years following the second world war, building on the war-related aerospace and electronics enterprises clustered around Stanford University (29). What in 1940 had been a peaceful agricultural valley with a population of 175 000 became one of the fastest growing urban areas in the USA and one of the densest concentrations of high technology enterprises in the world, to reach a population of 1¼ million in 1980. The region's dynamic growth was associated with the birth of the semiconductor industry; this involved a remarkable series of spin-outs originating ultimately in the Shockley Transistor Company (established in 1955 by one of the inventors of the transistor); the growth of such well known companies as Hewlett Packard (founded in Palo Alto in 1938) and Fairchild Semiconductor (1957); and also establishment in the county of major R&D facilities by Lockheed, IBM, ITT and others. By the end of the 1970s, there were some 35 companies each with more than 1 000 employees in the county, and employment in the high technology sector overall amounted to perhaps one quarter of total employment.

4.68 Given these origins of Silicon Valley, the comparison with Cambridge in 1984 would have to be the Valley in say 1960, certainly not 1984. Further, there was a period of some 25 years between the first significant developments in Silicon Valley and 'take-off' that occurred in the early 1960s in terms of frequency of new company formation, and absolute scale of growth; Cambridge is perhaps approaching such 'take-off' only now.

4.69 Time - or more strictly the age of the phenomenon in each location - is clearly not the only reason for the difficulty in making comparisons. The Silicon Valley experience – fuelled by massive federal R&D and other expenditures on aerospace and defence from the second world war onwards – is clearly of an absolute scale and speed of growth that could not be matched in Britain. Further differences lie in the industrial spread of the high technology companies – Silicon Valley being heavily concentrated on electronics (semiconductors originally), Cambridge much more widely distributed as seen earlier in this chapter – and in the rapid movement by the Silicon Valley companies into volume production while the Cambridge companies have so far remained concentrated in research, design and development (see further, next chapter).

4.70 The universities in both locations have played profoundly important roles. Later chapters will explore the many different ways in which, largely indirectly and subtly, the University in Cambridge, has exercised a long-term influence on the whole form and style of the phenomenon. Stanford's influence derives, perhaps more distinctly, from its consciously having set out after the war to become, along with MIT, one of the national centres of excellence in teaching and research in electronics and related disciplines. To stimulate the 'community of interest between (itself) and local industry', in the early 1950s the University also established alongside the campus Stanford industrial park, the first and probably most famous and successful of all science parks.

4.71 Interestingly, however, Stanford has had a far lower incidence of spin-out company formation than Cambridge. In the period 1960–69 there were only four such cases in Stanford (4); by contrast in the 1974–84 period there were 29 new companies formed by Cambridge University members in the Cambridge area. In Silicon Valley (far more than in Cambridge) spin-outs from existing companies have been the predominant source of new company formation; for instance, between 1959 and 1979 Fairchild Semiconductors spawned no fewer than 50 new enterprises in Santa Clara County (29).

4.72 In some respects the MIT/Route 128 phenomenon is rather more akin to Cambridge than is Stanford/Silicon Valley. It is of course older and on a far larger scale than Cambridge – a recent estimate puts the number of high technology firms in Boston at 1 350, employing a total of some 130 000 people (30). But as in Cambridge the sectoral distribution of the companies is quite widespread, and associated with this there is in addition to MIT a large and multidisciplinary research complex (some of it in federal establishments) in the area. MIT too has been a prolific source of spin-outs – some 160 companies between 1947 and 1967 (28) – as has the Lincoln radiation laboratory.

4.73 There are other university locations where there is also a concentration of high technology industry, but nothing yet on the scale of Silicon Valley and Route 128. And, at least in terms of the number of companies, there are evidently few locations that can match Cambridge too. For instance, Research Triangle Park in North Carolina (which is now nearly 30 years old and which draws in three universities and houses several federal and state research establishments) is said to have fewer than 150 companies (30). Austin (Texas) –

in which a major push, based on the local university, is under way to promote high technology activity – has about the same number.

4.74 There are other very large concentrations of high technology industry in the United States, but not so closely associated with universities. In some instances there appears to be no university involvement at all. In the Baltimore–Washington area, for example, large clusters of high technology firms are developing around a number of different federal facilities. Thus, in one county in Maryland, biotechnology firms are being drawn to the National Institute of Health and the Food and Drug Administration, and elsewhere in the state telecommunications and computer firms are being attracted to the National Security Agency and the Goddard Space Flight Centre.

4.75 Outside the United States, so far as we are aware, there are as yet no developments comparable in scale or form to what has been described earlier in this chapter about Cambridge. Chalmers Institute of Technology in Sweden is proving a fertile source of new firms (18), but the scale so far is still very small. Berlin is said to have quite a large number of new technology based firms, and a study is soon to be mounted to document this. But generally speaking, in all those countries (in western Europe, plus Japan, Canada and Australia) where promotion of advanced technology new firms has recently become a significant aim, it is true to say that the opportunities lie in the future rather than have yet been achieved.

FACTORS CAUSING AND SHAPING THE CAMBRIDGE PHENOMENON

INTRODUCTION

5.1   This chapter seeks to 'explain' the phenomenon described in the previous two chapters. It thus builds on the historical picture presented in chapter 2, but is analytical rather than purely descriptive.

WHAT IS THE PHENOMENON?

5.2   We are now in a position to venture a 'definition' of the phenomenon. No single or simple statement will suffice, and so the following are the distinctive characteristics that collectively make up the phenomenon:

(a) the presence in and immediately around Cambridge of a large number of high technology companies, mainly in the computing hardware and software, scientific instruments and electronics industries, and increasingly also in biotechnology;

(b) within this sector a very high proportion of young, small, independent and indigenous companies, and correspondingly a low proportion of subsidiary operations of large companies based elsewhere;

(c) a long record of high technology company formation in the area. This proceeded at a very modest rate until the 1960s when there was a slight increase in activity, followed by a further increase in the early-mid 1970s and a very substantial increase in the late 1970s which shows no sign of abating;

(d) the tendency for the high technology firms to be engaged in research-design-development activities or in small volume high value production. As a corollary there is an absence of large-scale production undertaken by the firms themselves (such volume production as there is being sub-contracted elsewhere);

(e) the many direct and indirect links that can be traced between these firms and the University and associated research complex, and also between the firms themselves.

5.3   As already observed, the high technology business scene in Cambridge is continually changing. A number of new developments are now taking place – such as the very rapid growth of a few of the local companies and the establishment in the area of prestigious research and other projects by international companies – that will profoundly influence the future shape and direction of the phenomenon. We speculate in chapter 8 about the future, but in this chapter we are concerned to explain the origins of the phenomenon and how it has evolved to date.

ORIGINS AND FORMATIVE INFLUENCES

5.4   Has the phenomenon been 'demand-led' or 'supply-pushed'? To put this another way, have the Cambridge companies been operating in markets with very strong demand; or have they, irrespective of the strength of demand, been able to supply their goods and services more competitively than others, taking into account not just relative prices but also technology, design and other factors?

5.5   In seeking to answer these questions it is helpful to distinguish between:

(a) market factors, ie to do with the demand for goods and services that Cambridge could supply;

(b) factors that constituted a general preconditioning effect in Cambridge, thereby laying the base for Cambridge enterprises competitively to supply these goods and services;

(c) a further set of supply factors, made up of particular and recent decisions and events, that were of specific and direct significance in stimulating formation and growth of the Cambridge firms.

5.6   These three categories are not so clearly separable as might first appear, on three counts. First, demand and supply factors are interlinked and the causation can go in either direction. It is well understood that in advanced technological industry in particular, supply tends to create demand. On this basis, in the case of particular products it may be that it is Cambridge's ability to supply that itself generates the market for those products and it is not a question of Cambridge firms facing a 'given' external demand for their output.

5.7   An important point follows from this. Whether it is because they are creating new markets or competing successfully against other firms in existing markets, the critical issue is to do with why Cambridge firms have such a well developed supply capability in the sectors in which they operate. It is for this reason that our study focuses attention on the supply rather than the demand side of the overall phenomenon.

5.8   Second, there has been a significant incidence of inter-trading between the local companies. A prime contractor's ability to compete in external markets (his supply capability) thus becomes translated into demand for the sub-contractors' services; and the increased output from both local companies is thus a consequence of both demand and supply factors.

5.9 Third, the two categories of supply factors – the general preconditioning and the specific precipitating – are themselves often overlapping. Assignment of a particular influence to one or the other category may thus sometimes seem a little arbitrary. Nevertheless, as in the demand-supply distinction, we feel the classification remains useful.

DEMAND FACTORS

5.10 In some fields, of which computer aided design and scanning electron microscopy would be excellent early examples, Cambridge know-how has made a vital contribution to helping open up new markets. How those markets have evolved, along with how they have interacted with other technologies and markets, has in turn created new demand pressures and supply opportunities. Later generation firms in the same fields may well thus have rather more specific and identifiable market gaps to fill than was previously the case.

5.11 The interaction of developments in the CAD and microcomputer fields illustrates the point. CAD technology 'took off' commercially in the late 1970s, microcomputer technology in the early 1980s: in both cases Cambridge know-how has played a distinctive role. There are now new market opportunities emerging and there are, for instance, several Cambridge firms developing specialised software and hardware to supply sophisticated CAD on micros.

5.12 Market factors of a peculiarly local and different kind have been important too. Establishment of Pye and Cambridge Instruments in the last century illustrate the point. There was demand from the University for specialised instruments but no local industry to supply – hence a market niche for a new company to fill. This pattern of specialised local demand creating new markets and inducing supply from existing and new local firms has continued and increased; though now it is the larger companies like Acorn Computers rather than the University that play this primary role.

5.13 Acorn illustrates another favourable market factor. The market – or more often individual major clients (in Acorn's case, the BBC) – has 'picked up' some of the companies and enabled them to expand at a pace and to a scale that could not otherwise even have been anticipated. Similarly, the market has often been 'forgiving' too, in that it has been patient while the firms have overcome advanced technical problems or even simply made mistakes.

5.14 The general point to be made is this. Market circumstances, whether growing in aggregate or becoming more specialised or both, have been favourable for a sizeable proportion of Cambridge companies. Thus, while it is justified to turn attention very much to Cambridge's 'supply capability', it is important to remember that the relevant markets have been expanding and have in no way yet constituted a constraint on growth of local high technology company sector.

GENERAL, PRECONDITIONING SUPPLY FACTORS

5.15 These factors can themselves be conveniently divided into two groups: those peculiar to Cambridge and those of a wider national or regional character and applicability. The latter category is discussed first.

5.16 The rapid economic growth of East Anglia from the 1960s onwards and the major improvements in the late 1970s to the region's strategic communications network were discussed in chapter 2. They have contributed materially to business developments in Cambridge; the transport improvements have been especially important recently in making Cambridge an increasingly efficient and sophisticated business location, for the reasons discussed in the previous chapter.

5.17 A further set of general preconditioning factors began to operate in the 1970s. These were to do with the increasingly favourable national environment for small firms that began to emerge around 1970. After a long history of being disfavoured in terms of government policies and public attitudes, small firms started becoming both acceptable and respectable. A combination of a 'small is beautiful' philosophy and a realisation that very large companies did not offer a sufficient solution to the country's economic problems resulted both in more individuals being inclined to 'do their own business thing', and in government and other institutions introducing measures to promote start-up and growth of small firms.

5.18 These factors fortuitously coincided with certain technological developments especially in computing. Massive strides were made in electronics and computer design, resulting in a steep fall in hardware costs. This in turn made it easier for small firms to enter the burgeoning fields of computer applications and new hardware development. The 'ripening' of computer technology starting in the 1970s in a way that was suitable for commercial exploitation by small firms across a wide range of industries has been an important factor in Cambridge (as it has been elsewhere for firms in these sectors).

5.19 In addition to the above national, regional and technological factors there have been general but Cambridge-specific factors that have helped create a fertile environment in Cambridge for new technology based firms.

Cambridge University

5.20 The first and most obvious of these factors is to do with Cambridge University itself. Exactly what makes up the University is difficult to describe satisfactorily; a few facts were given in chapter 2, as well as an attempt to describe the place of the University in Cambridge as a city. But it is not so much what it is in a literal sense that matters; rather it is its general style and its excellence in many subjects, notably including both the physical and life sciences.

5.21 In respect of the University's academic excellence, a virtuous circle operates. Its prestige and reputation plus the presence of recognised leaders in the subjects concerned attract high quality undergraduates; the latter – who stand out for their intellectual liveliness and speed of working – themselves attract high calibre staff and stimulate them to be even better; this in turn ensures a continuing high quality of undergraduates. The interaction between faculty and students is widely regarded by the former as a very special feature of Cambridge relative to most other universities in Britain. Similarly the University is able to attract amongst the very best research students.

5.22 It is not easy to document satisfactorily these matters of quality. One can see from the University's own data on the undergraduates that educational attainments at school tend to be high; and it is common knowledge that the average entry qualifications are exceptionally high. But comparative data for other universities are not publicly available, and in any event pre-university scholastic performance is an imperfect guide to what we are trying to assess. There is, similarly, no data available that could rigorously demonstrate the relative quality of the University's output of graduates.

5.23 Nevertheless, there are three strong pointers.

The first is the so-called 'peer review' published in December 1982 by the Times Higher Educational Supplement. Heads of departments in selected disciplines in all those UK universities and polytechnics which offered the subject concerned were asked which they judged the best five departments in the country in teaching and research terms. The responses were scored and the departments ranked accordingly. In the science and engineering subjects covered (chemistry, physics, architecture, civil engineering) Cambridge achieved top rank in both research and teaching, except in one instance in the latter category where it was placed second.

5.24 The second pointer is to do with the allocation of overseas research student awards. This is a scheme, established in 1979, whereby the Department of Education and Science contributes to the fees of selected overseas postgraduate students doing research in British universities. It operates on a competitive basis and its selection criteria are to do with academic excellence only; consequently the award-winners can be considered the best of the best, and the universities they enter can be similarly credited. In the four years that the scheme has been running Cambridge has emerged as by far the most successful institution: for the 1984 academic year, for instance, 97% of its applications were successful, and the number of its awards represented 20% of the national total (by contrast Cambridge's share of the national university research student population is approximately 6%).

5.25 The third indicator is to do with the allocation of public sector research funds. While comprehensive data are not available, the University Grants Committee advised us that Cambridge had generally been better funded for research than the average university, both by the UGC and the research councils. Our own analysis of data on expenditure by the Science and Engineering Research Council (SERC), which accounts for the giant's share of total research monies, confirmed this: in subjects such as the biological sciences, physics and materials Cambridge has been a very prominent (sometimes dominant) recipient of funds.

5.26 The University has a long history of scientific research. This goes back at least to Newton, though it is really to the 1840s (when a natural sciences tripos was introduced) that the growth of its modern strength can be traced. This history is notable not just for some remarkable scientific achievements but also for a few but strategically vital policies adopted at different times which ensured the continuing vitality of the institution's scientific research in changing outside circumstances. Among these policies have been:

(a) a decision in the 1890s to admit graduates of other universities as research students (which soon resulted in outstanding outsiders – Rutherford in physics would be an excellent early example – coming in and making distinguished contributions);

(b) a decision in the 1920s to place special emphasis on developing a research excellence in Cambridge and to do so by strengthening the faculty structure rather than the colleges. (As a consequence departmental research has occupied a more prominent position in Cambridge as compared with Oxford, while Oxford has retained a more highly developed collegiate structure);

(c) the Mott report of 1969, referred to frequently elsewhere in this study, which firmly identified the interests of long-term research which industrial application and whose philosophy has continued to inform the strategic thinking of the University authorities in these matters;

(d) a willingness to back strong individuals in building up departments or specialist units in their particular fields, thereby creating "steeples of excellence" to quote Frederick Terman's famous phrase about what distinguishes great universities.* Clerk Maxwell in physics in the last century, and in this century Bernal in crystallography, Bragg in physics, Hopkins in biochemistry, Baker in engineering, and Wilkes in computing, are among the many examples;

(e) conversely a willingness to cut off lines of research when it seemed clear that the discipline had reached its natural end and in this way to concentrate resources on new and more fruitful fields;

(f) a deliberate policy of attracting to Cambridge, and where possible even physically housing them, specialist national research units sponsored by the Medical and Agricultural Research Councils. Well known amongst these are the ARC Commonwealth institute of agricultural biology and the MRC laboratory of molecular biology.

---

*Terman was the far-sighted electrical engineering professor at Stanford who later became dean, provost and vice president of the University and who played a central role in cultivating a 'community of technical scholars' in Palo Alto after the second world war.

5.27 The University's research excellence in a number of fields directly relevant to the Cambridge phenomenon was noted in earlier chapters. Chapter 2 mentioned the links between local instrument engineering firms and work, in both the Cavendish and in the engineering department, on scanning electron microscopy and other electron optical techniques as well as other surface analytical techniques; these are elaborated in box 5.1. Research work in the biosciences will be conveniently discussed in a later section. On a rather different note, but nevertheless highly germane because of its persuasive influence on many other disciplines, is the history of development of the computer laboratory (see box 5.2).

5.28 Quite apart from the sheer quality of the University is the matter of its 'style'. There is an assuredness – born of a mix of a long and distinguished history, substantial resources and a sense of uniqueness in the University's special setting in Cambridge as a town – that encourages people to think long and not to feel pressured by immediate events. There is, among dons and students alike, an ethos of independence, individualism and self-confidence. To the outsider not familiar with the style, it may seem complacent and exclusive; but that is to misunderstand the origins and to underestimate the underlying motivation and ability.

5.29 There are four further aspects of Cambridge University, all quite distinctive, which have exercised a profoundly general influence on the phenomenon.

5.30 The first of these derives from the University's collegiate structure, which was described briefly in chapter 2. The vital features here are four-fold, all interrelated:

(a) the autonomy, strength and sheer number of the colleges, alongside what is a very small central administration for the University, make for a diffuse and informal system in which decisions and decentralised and maximum reliance is placed on the individual;

(b) the great majority of University faculty members also are college fellows. Although the University is, contractually and financially, the principal employer, fellows have real obligations in and typically strong attachments towards their colleges, and in practice a departmental head can exercise only modest influence on his staff members' day-to-day activities. This is generally the case, but especially so in large departments like engineering;

BOX 5.1 THE UNIVERSITY AND THE DEVELOPMENT OF ELECTRON-OPTICAL INSTRUMENTS

The origins of electron-optical instrument technology, as a means of measuring basic physico-chemical characteristics of various materials, go back to Germany in the mid-1920s. Despite extensive work there as well as in France and the USA over the next 20 years, and although the conceptual problems were essentially solved, it proved impossible to design and make instruments of sufficiently high resolution and reliability; and it was not until the technology was returned to at Cambridge after the war that significant breakthroughs were achieved and a variety of instruments successfully constructed (13, 25).

There were two roughly parallel but interacting developments in the University that led directly to this success. One was in the Cavendish where since 1946 V E Cosslett had been pursuing research in electron optics for in situ analysis of metals and alloys. In the mid-1950s an electron probe X-ray microanalyser was successfully built in the Cavendish. The instrument came to the attention of Tube Investment Limited's research laboratories based at Hinxton Hall some 10 miles south of Cambridge. The company recruited Peter Duncumb (who had been responsible for the earlier work in the Cavendish, and who is now head of the Hinxton Hall laboratories) to make a properly engineered version of the instrument, which was achieved and became operational in 1958. This design shortly afterwards became the basis of an instrument (called Microscan) made commercially by Cambridge Instruments, which sold outstandingly successfully over the next few years mostly to Germany and the USA before being discontinued.

The second source of electron-optical know-how in the University was in the engineering department. C W Oatley (who later became professor of electrical engineering) joined the department in 1945 in order to build up a teaching and research capability in electronics. Encouraged by research work taking place in the Cavendish and motivated to move away from radar on which he had concentrated for some years, Oatley instigated a research programme in scanning electron microscopy. An outstanding series of doctoral students enabled a microscope to be designed and successively improved in the 1950s and 1960s, and also a variety of other electron-optical methods to be pioneered.

The work in the engineering department had a strongly applied orientation – by the mid-1950s a wide range of applications in biology, metallurgy and electronics had been successfully demonstrated. The department also had an outstanding workshop and was able itself to design and build very complex, high precision equipment. A consequence of these two features of the department was that it was possible for K C A Smith (who had been Oatley's second research student in the field, and who has remained in the department as a reader) to take a complete scanning electron microscope made in the de-

partment to Canada in 1958 for application in the pulp and paper industry.

At that early stage it had been envisaged that if production of the microscope appeared commercially viable it would be taken up by Associated Electrical Industries (AEI) who had shipped Smith's instrument to Canada. However, AEI were sceptical about the size of the market for such sophisticated apparatus and, after one unhappy experience with supplying an instrument to the Cavendish, decided not to continue in scanning microscopy.

Members of the University's engineering department nevertheless remained convinced that there was a substantial market. Two in particular – Smith, and W C Nixon who had earlier worked under Cosslett in the Cavendish and from around 1960 became increasingly involved in the supervision of research in electron optics as Oatley was pre-occupied with administrative duties – were anxious to see the instrument made locally. They were able to interest Cambridge Instruments to do so, especially as some of the components for the Microscan (see above) and the Stereoscan (as the first version of the scanning microscope came to be called) could be expected to be the same. The company commenced experimental work on the scanning microscope in 1961, and in 1962 a full-scale development programme was launched under A D G Stewart, who had recently been a research student under Oatley in the engineering department.

The first commercial models of the Stereoscan were produced by Cambridge Instruments in 1965. Its success (despite a high price, then around £20 000) exceeded all expectations. By the end of 1967 more than 100 units had been installed, mostly in Britain, Germany and the United States; in 1968 alone over 100 instruments were sold. The Queen's Award for technological innovation in respect of the Stereoscan was granted in 1967, and for export performance in 1970. Cambridge Instruments have continued with development of the instrument, which is currently produced in its sixth version.

A more general consequence of the extensive association highlighted above between the engineering department and the local instrument engineering industry was stimulation of awareness among the academic staff and their research students of the possibilities for commercial application of their know-how and specific inventions. In the 1960s, for instance, numerous patents in the electron optics field were taken out by people such as Nixon and Smith, who were also active in consultancy. The know-how has also found commercial application through establishment of several local companies by former students of the department – Lintech Instruments and Cambridge Mass Spectrometry both on the science park, and Cambridge Scanning at Bar Hill.

(c) each college constitutes essentially an informal society of its own, embracing a wide variety of academic disciplines and cultural and ethnic origins. The colleges thus provide a unique environment for social and inter-disciplinary contact within the entire academic and research community, far more effectively than is achievable in a non-collegiate university;

(d) the colleges, rather than the University, encourage connections with the outside world. Alumni return to their colleges not their departments, for social and other purposes. Most colleges have a system of outside visiting fellows; the latter have no special duties but because of their experience and connections in industry, government or wherever are expected to add to the tone and breadth of college life and perhaps to exercise influence as may be appropriate from time to time. A number of the principals in the local high technology companies hold such fellowships. Finally, the college bursars are constantly in touch with the local professional and business community and with major outside bodies such as financial institutions in the City of London; they are thus uniquely placed to provide links between academic and business interests, and also to encourage use of the college's own resources (eg investment capital, premises for start-ups) to support local high technology companies.

5.31 The second distinctive feature of the University – well illustrated by the small number of permanent staff in the computer laboratory – is the high proportion of teaching and research staff who are on short fixed-term contracts or have no expectation of tenure. In December 1982, for instance, of the total of 1734 staff almost 49% fell into this category. This situation arises not because tenure is especially difficult to get at Cambridge compared with elsewhere but rather because of a long-standing reluctance on the part of the authorities to build up a large 'overhead' and equally a recognition that they could take a strong line on long-term appointments because of the competition for the available places. To illustrate the point differently: the average age of appointment of a lecturer is 34 (compared with the mid-20s for most other universities), and of an assistant lecturer 29 (this post is not commonly found elsewhere but the role would typically be played by people in their early 20s).

5.32 The consequence of this appointments policy is the presence in Cambridge at any one time of numerous research workers who do not see long-term careers for themselves in the University. Because a significant number tend to want to stay in Cambridge (see later), their only means of doing so is to go into industry, which for a number of individuals up to now has meant starting a new business themselves.

5.33 A broadly similar situation arises in the case of research students, although the underlying causes are quite different. Postgraduate numbers have been about 2 500 in recent years; at any one time a proportion will be looking for occasional work and consequently they constitute a sizeable and excellent pool of part-time employees for the young companies.

5.34 The third particular feature of the University concerns the terms of employment of staff. Most other universities have a uniform and highly specific structure for all employment contracts, with little if any margin for flexibility. Cambridge by contrast has a variety of rather loose contractual relationships which place rather more emphasis on academic staff living close to the city and seldom being absent during term time (arising out of the commitment to having a genuine community of teachers and scholars) than on formal job descriptions. The essence of the contractual relationship is that, in accordance with the basic principles of academic freedom, academics are expected to devote themselves to advancement of their subject, to give instruction to students, and to promote the interests of the University as a place of education and research. The consequence of this, along with the collegiate structure discussed above and also reinforced by the considerations of the next paragraph, is that Cambridge academics have a great deal of freedom and feel treated as responsible and independent individuals.

5.35 The final distinctive aspect is the authorities' policy towards commercial exploitation of academics's know-how and links with industry generally. In essence the policy is to stand back and, provided their academic tasks are satisfactorily performed, to leave it to the individual to decide how he wants to spend the rest of his time and whether and in what manner he wants to engage in outside work. In the applied sciences in particular there is a natural presumption that staff, because of their quality, will be involved in consultancy or other such work.

5.36 Similarly, the administration has a permissive attitude to the ownership of intellectual property rights.

These vest in the individual academics not the University or any other party unless the research contract which generated the know-how stipulates otherwise –in any event there is no automatic presumption that these should vest in the University, as is the case at probably most other universities.

5.37 The corollary to these policies is that the University as an institution accepts no legal liability in respect of any outside work done by its staff. The risk is entirely that of the academics involved, either as individuals or as a business entity if they happen to have set themselves up in a formal way.

5.38 These liberal policies have contributed directly and indirectly to the Cambridge phenomenon. They have helped create an environment in which industrial links of all kinds have been allowed to flourish without fear of sanction or bureaucratic intervention, as too easily can happen in a rigid even if well-intentioned regime.

5.39 The matter is of profound interest to the future of university-industry relationships in Britain more generally, and is discussed in this wider context in chapter 7.

Local research and technological institutes
5.40 There is, as noted before, a concentration of research and technological institutes, in both the public and private sectors, in the vicinity of Cambridge. Some are quite independent of the University, others quite closely associated with it and in some cases even housed in University departments. Virtually all of them originally located in the area because of the University.

5.41 For a variety of historic reasons, some to do with the importance of East Anglia in the agricultural sector, there is a notable concentration of establishments in such fields as plant breeding and other crop-related research, animal physiology and nutrition. There is also the MRC laboratory of molecular biology, whose work grew essentially out of the Cavendish. This laboratory has played a leading role in deciphering the genetic code of DNA (made famous in the book "The Double Helix") and in developing monoclonal antibodies, both of which developments have transformed biosciences over the past 20 years. It has produced an astonishingly high quality of research output and numbers of Nobel laureates. Among the famous names are Perutz, Kendrew, Crick, Watson, Sanger (who has won the Nobel prize twice), Klug and Milstein.

5.42 In addition to the bioscience research institutions, there is a number of other technological establishments notably in materials science and metallurgy. Tube Investment's national R&D laboratory at Hinxton Hall was mentioned in chapter 2. Another example is that of the Welding Institute at Abington whose choice of location can be traced back partly to collaborative work with the University's engineering department.

5.43 To date, while they have had numerous and fruitful links with the University, these various research bodies have played only a modest direct role in the Cambridge phenomenon in the particular sense of being a breeding ground for new high technology companies. But their role is becoming increasingly significant for two main reasons.

5.44 First, in the biosciences in particular, there has recently been an increasing incidence of high technology companies in Cambridge; prior to 1981 there were only three companies in biotechnology – now there are nearly 20. Moreover, two of the new companies in Cambridge have as their basic aim the commercialisation of selected projects undertaken in the research laboratories (though not confined to those in Cambridge). Hence an increasing number of new ventures should materialise in the future, with a good chance of some of them being located in Cambridge.

5.45 Second, the presence of the research bodies, with their complements of highly qualified staff, is now being recognised by large companies as augmenting the University's strengths and hence making Cambridge an additionally attractive location for part of their own operations. The staff are also seen as potential recruits, especially as public expenditure on research gets squeezed – already there is evidence of this happening. Again these are quite recent trends and mostly in the biosciences field. There are two main categories of such new projects:
   (a) establishment by outside firms, all so far being from overseas, of marketing/distribution activities perhaps with limited production and R&D and also with a 'listening post' function into the Cambridge laboratories;
   (b) strengthening of research activity of existing organisations in Cambridge, because Cambridge is seen as an outstanding and internationally recognised base for such work.

```
┌─────────────────────────────────────────────────────────────────────────────┐
│                                                                             │
│        ┌─ BOX 5.2  DEVELOPMENT OF COMPUTING IN CAMBRIDGE ─┐                  │
```

The computer laboratory's origins go back to 1937 when a group was established in the university to undertake research in analogue computing (this makes it the oldest department in the country). The team was dispersed during the war and only one member, Maurice Wilkes, returned to Cambridge in 1946 and was given responsibility for building up computing in the University. Wilkes had the opportunity to learn the new computer ideas at the More School in Philadelphia and, because of the war-time experience he had gained at the Telecommunications Research Laboratory, could at once set about building a digital computer which was completed in mid-1949.

Wilkes' interest was not so much on the hardware per se. His aim was to construct a machine good enough to enable programming development, and after 1949 he concentrated on software development using mathematical sub-routines. His far-sighted perception was that the computer would find application in a very wide range of disciplines and so he set about fostering in the University an appreciation of digital computers and their implications for different fields of research. To this end he introduced in the early 1950s a variety of short courses for postgraduates and others; modern versions of these courses still run today.

Wilkes' vigorous promotion of the application of computers found a receptive audience among his academic colleagues in Cambridge. There seems little doubt that in several fields (notably molecular biology, computer aided design in architecture and engineering, and certain scientific instruments) Cambridge was at the leading edge in the use of computers. There was an early excitement about applying computers in new directions which continues unabated in the computer laboratory to this day.

Digital computers were being built at a number of other establishments in Britain in the late 1940s; the developments were largely independent of one another and were also rather different in their emphases. Notable amongst them was the project at Manchester University where, in contrast to Cambridge, the whole orientation was towards the continual enhancement of hardware technology and processor architecture (16). Manchester, which is usually credited with having the world's first demonstrable stored-program operational digital computer, maintained its research emphasis on the hardware side and, responding to the realisation that by the mid-

1950s Britain had fallen far behind the United States in high-performance computers, in collaboration with Ferranti (later International Computers and Tabulators and then International Computers Limited) successfully completed the Atlas computer in 1962 which was at that time among the world's most powerful computers.

In the same year Ferranti provided Cambridge University with some units of Atlas hardware on special terms in return for assistance in developing a simpler version of Atlas. The result was development of the Titan machine – it was a slightly modified version of this called Atlas 2, which was installed in the Computer Aided Design Centre in Cambridge in 1968 (see box 2.2). Initially there was a close association between the computing laboratory and the CADCentre. But once it became clear that CAD problems no longer were the special domain of computer scientists but needed in particular the skills of the mechanical engineer or architect, and also because of a shortage of academic posts, the laboratory withdrew from formal involvement in CAD.

The computer laboratory has been primarily research-oriented throughout its life. It has also remained small; in the mid-1970s one of the (probably unintended) effects of this was to stimulate a number of individuals who could not get permanent posts and who wanted to stay in Cambridge to set up in business locally. In 1983 there were 15 full-time staff, an increase of 50% over the previous year because of the favourable allocation of 'new blood' IT posts. There were also 11 externally funded senior researchers and 30 students working towards higher degrees. The department's influence is out of all proportion to these modest numbers.

The laboratory operates a very relaxed and open-door policy towards collaboration with industry. The know-how in the 'Cambridge ring', the local area network developed in the laboratory, was given to several companies simultaneously; the real pay-back was expected in kind in terms of future collaboration though contributions towards defraying the costs of developing the ring were welcomed. A number of local companies contribute towards an 'industrial fund' in recognition of the benefits they derive from the laboratory. There is a close relationship with a number of computer firms, both locally and further afield, and several staff members hold outside directorships.

5.46 These developments have particular implications for the future of the phenomenon and will be discussed further in chapter 8.

Public expenditure on research

5.47 It is interesting to restate some of the points made earlier in this chapter from a somewhat different angle. Public research expenditure has been a fundamentally important preconditioning factor in Cambridge.

5.48 Computer aided design provides a clear example of this. The long history of support involved in building up the computer laboratory, together with two key research projects of the late 1960s (the then Ministry of Technology establishment of the Computer Aided Design Centre and the then Science Research Council's support for seminal CAD work in the computer laboratory) laid the base for expansion of the CAD-related small firms sector from the mid-1970s onwards.

5.49 The very recent and prospective developments in the biotechnology sector reflect the same point. Their origins lie inter alia in Medical Research Council funded work starting in the 1950s. It is interesting to note, as in computing, the long gestation period before the original research finds direct commercial application.

5.50 In the United States the significance of public research expenditure in these respects has been well recognised (13). Both Stanford and MIT, as well as the surrounding research institutes and high technology companies, have been major recipients of such funds from the second world war onwards. It has been estimated that the Californian economy alone received some US $35 billion of defence related expenditures in the war (21), and in both areas it is possible to trace the impact of public outlays directly and indirectly on the continuing development of local high technology industry (11, 27).

Role of the Cambridge science park

5.51 The Cambridge science park (CSP) was in effect the first physical manifestation of the recommendations of the Mott committee (see chapters 2 and 4). Yet it is fair to say that, although it was available for occupation from quite an early date (1973) it played no more than a very minor role in stimulating the phenomenon and in constituting a focal point for high technology industrial activity in the area. This situation has now changed quite substantially, and CSP is finally established as a critical element in sustaining and enhancing the phenomenon.

5.52 There have been five components to this growing role:

(a) CSP began in the late 1970s speculatively to provide small units of good but not over-expensive quality on reasonably short terms. These have proved admirably suited to the needs of already established local small firms requiring more space and/or seeking to move 'up market' as they develop. More recently there have also been a reasonable number of brand-new starts on CSP;

(b) similarly, CSP has so far been easily the principal location in the area offering a high quality property environment in all respects to sizeable, prestige projects of international companies and to substantial local firms with equally demanding property requirements. (It has, correspondingly, offered the most expensive industrial property available to date);

(c) academic-industry links and inter-company contact (which arise more frequently and fruitfully than on a conventional industrial estate) have become steadily more important;

(d) CSP, as perhaps the most successful university science park in Europe to date, has become a visible and prestigious symbol to the outside world that high technology industry is flourishing in Cambridge. The fact of a high degree of international interest in CSP has given both confidence and a sense of status to the local high technology sector in general and also a stimulus to the park's tenant small firms, constantly under external scrutiny, to perform better. A highly visible prestigiously located firm, perhaps written about in the national or international press, is in a very different position psychologically from one anonymously housed in converted premises in the side streets of Cambridge;

(e) as a counterpart to the previous point, CSP has come to constitute a no less significant symbol to the 'inside' world (the University) of the success of Cambridge as a location for high technology industry and of the easy compatibility (even ignoring the benefits) of this industry with Cambridge as a university town. The science park is thus much better known, and has been more effective, than the Mott report in indicating to the academic community the commitment of powerful bodies in the University to stimulating links with science-based industry.

5.53 Many factors have gone into making up CSP's growing success and integral role in evolution of Cambridge science-based industry. The above discussion has stressed the property aspects. Arguably of no less significance, especially in relation to the technology transfer process, is the manner in which the whole development has been planned and managed. One must not be deceived by the informal and light-touch methods used for cultivating academic-industry links – they fit well with the style of the University and they carry behind them the full weight and multiple scientific connections of one of the most powerful of all the colleges.

5.54 Further discussion in general terms of the role of a science park in fostering university-industry links is given in chapter 7.

Industrial history and structure

5.55 Cambridge's short and modest industrial past has had a number of particular features that have indirectly had a powerful influence on the phenomenon. First, the very fact of this limited history has meant that industrial market opportunities, often generated by the University, have been readily identifiable and, in the absence both of local competition and of firms to whom know-how could readily be licensed, have been open to new firm penetration.

5.56 Second, within the industrial sector the fact that there has never been heavy industry, or industries in which large plants and large unionised labour forces have been prominent, has helped create a labour market and a general psychological attitude in which flexibility and individualism have never been suppressed. A history of low wages – due to the long dominance of the agricultural and low-level services sectors, reinforced by the early industrial employers – and a generally low penetration of trade unionism have contributed to the effective functioning of the labour market.

5.57 Third, a pool of skilled manual and technical labour has been created which has been of incalculable benefit to the small high technology firms that have started up in the more recent past. This has been particularly evident in the instruments and electronics sectors, and interestingly also in other fields such as printing and publishing where the long-standing skills have found ready application in software publications and technical literature more generally.

The special character of Cambridge as a town

5.58 Cambridge exercises an unusual hold over people who have studied and worked there, and of course over those who still do. It is not one single attribute, though most people have their particular preference. Rather it is a remarkable amalgam of the physical form of the city in the central area; the beauty of the colleges and other mediaeval buildings and the atmosphere they generate; the profound even if indirect influence exercised by the University on so many aspects of life, felt all the more because of the relatively small size of the city; the liveliness of the place, with street events and fairs and also music, drama and other cultural activities throughout the year; the high standard of the local schools, which is partly due to a desire by graduate teachers to stay on in the area; and perhaps above all from the point of view of this study, the functioning of numerous interlocking networks of talented, influential and accessible individuals, which makes for informal, congenial and efficient business dealings.

5.59 The relatively small size of Cambridge, combined with the absence of large-scale industries and dominant companies, has had an important bearing on much of how it operates as a social and business centre. There is no question of the University's becoming engulfed and inconspicuous within a large metropolis. Likewise it is easy for people to know what is going on in those areas of life that interest them; and the fact that people like Sinclair, Curry, and Hauser have become significant role models to many of the young entrepreneurs is facilitated by virtue of their being known to or at least reasonably regularly seen and recognised by the latter. Similarly, the robustness of the phenomenon – in that there have been no major business failures so far and that the bigger firms that have had unhappy episodes have all pulled through successfully – has directly exercised a positive psychological effect.

5.60 The small size and easy style of Cambridge have together had a consequence of a different sort. It has been much easier than it would in a large city for a 'critical mass' of high technology firms to be reached. This has allowed the firms to be noticed – in effect the phenomenon to be recognised – with the attendant benefits of practical support and generation of confidence among themselves. In Imperial College, say, these benefits are much harder to realise because the firms would be 'lost' (or at least highly dispersed) in London so that a critical mass would not readily be reached.

5.61 It would be wrong to maintain that Cambridge works harmoniously in all respects. The ancient tensions between town and gown cannot be expected to disappear suddenly. Similarly, the elitism and exclusiveness that exist in parts of the University have conditioned at least some of the 'networks' mentioned above and how they operate; it is unlikely to be easy for rank outsiders to get quickly onto these networks unless they have a special introduction.

5.62 Yet it is in these respects too that the high technology companies are coming to prove important. They are gradually constituting useful bridges between town and gown, academe and industry, and industry and the planning authorities; and the fact that these relationships have proved so fruitful is one of the reasons for creation of an environment in which high technology industry is flourishing.

5.63 It is for all these reasons that there has been living in Cambridge and its immediate surroundings such a high proportion (by UK standards) of people willing to set up in business for the first time, and finding it a fruitful environment in which to operate. These factors likewise explain the high geographic concentration of the companies in and around Cambridge itself.

SUPPLY FACTORS HAVING A DIRECT INFLUENCE IN STIMULATING THE PHENOMENON

5.64 It will be well evident by now that the Cambridge phenomenon must be viewed as a long-term development process, shaped by many external and internal factors. There is no simple causality, and no single factor that can properly be regarded in isolation from others – there is too much interaction between them, as well as mutual reinforcement, for such a simple model to apply.

5.65 Yet it is a valid question to ask: over and above the contextual, 'preconditioning' factors discussed above, have there been particular decisions or events that have directly stimulated the phenomenon? Put another way, are there factors that, if they had happened elsewhere, might have made an equivalent contribution in that other hypothetical place? It is an awkward question because the answers might be construed as implying a 'superior' role for the precipitating as opposed to the preconditioning factors.

5.66 With the above reservations in mind, we would identify the following factors as exercising a direct, stimulating influence on the phenomenon:

(a) the formation in 1960 of what is now Cambridge Consultants and the role they have played in spinning out new ventures and in setting a pattern for the ready flow of people between local companies;

(b) establishment by the government of the Computer Aided Design Centre in 1969 (see box 2.2 in chapter 2) and similarly the large number of spin-out businesses to which this too has given rise;

(c) the formation also in 1969 of Applied Research of Cambridge, a spin-out from the University's school of architecture which both gave practical help to young start-up companies in the early 1970s and also provided a visible and successful demonstration of a company formed by academics only;

(d) the Mott report of 1969 and its impact on attitudes in the University and the county planning authority towards having science-based industry in Cambridge;

(e) the formation of the Cambridge Computer Group in 1979 (now the Cambridge Technology Association – see box 5.3), which gave the emerging phenomenon an identity and made it visible, and also helped achieve the 'critical mass' vital to its self-sustaining growth;

(f) the lending policies adopted in the late 1970s by Barclays Bank which greatly increased the availability of debt finance for start-up and young companies in advanced technology (also see box 5.3 on the Cambridge Technology Association).

5.67 One can only speculate whether, if indeed these decisions and events had taken place elsewhere, even in the absence of the preconditioning that had been going on in Cambridge over a long period, there would have been the same end results. Or were they themselves peculiar to Cambridge in some way, and was it this Cambridge-specific feature that made them happen at all? By way of example, on this latter argument, it could be said that the CADCentre was not the first or only government-funded technology establishment to have an unsatisfactory interface with industry, but have any of the others been so important a source of successful spin-out companies?

5.68 There are clearly no easy answers to these and related questions. We suspect there is a Cambridge-specific element in some instances – where else in Britain in 1960 could an enterprise with the outrageous boldness of what became Cambridge Consultants have

┌───┐

BOX 5.3 CAMBRIDGE TECHNOLOGY ASSOCIATION

The Cambridge Technology Association (until recently called the Cambridge Computer Group) has its origins in a meeting called in July 1979 by Jack Lang of Topexpress Limited and Matthew Bullock who was an assistant manager in the Bene't Street, Cambridge branch of Barclays Bank. The association's founding purpose was to encourage greater cooperation and mutual support amongst young and small computer-related companies in and around Cambridge, and to work towards using their group strength to improve their purchasing and marketing power.

The origins of the group are interesting. Bullock, whose father is the well-known Oxford historian, had graduated in history from Cambridge in 1970 and then entered Barclays Bank in London. He kept close ties with Cambridge – partly through his older brother, a don in the school of architecture and a co-founder of Applied Research of Cambridge, and partly through other social connections – and in 1978 Barclays regional office based in Cambridge requested that he be posted to Bene't Street. It was felt that his particular background would make him especially effective in a university town like Cambridge.

Bullock soon became aware that a good number of computer-related businesses had recently started up whose founders had spun out of, or were still associated with, the University and other local research establishments. He became responsible for the accounts of some of them and gained direct experience of their start-up and early development problems. In this process he met Jack Lang (and his brother Charles of Shape Data Limited), and it was out of this that the decision was taken to set up an informal club for local computer-based firms.

The founding meeting took place in The Eagle, a well-known Cambridge pub, in July 1979. A total of 11 people representing nine young computer-based firms attended. The meeting identified, without difficulty, roughly another two dozen such local companies in computing and other high technology fields. A second meeting was held later in the year, at which some 35 companies each gave a short talk on themselves and there was also general discussion about how to develop the potential of the group.

While the group has probably had little if any material effect on performance of an individual enterprise, formation had five significant consequences. First, the individual companies were assisted in their own efforts – partly through meetings at which outside experts talked on topics of special concern to high technology companies, mostly through the psychological and practical benefits of having contact with a number of other similar companies at roughly the same stage of development.

Second, Barclays Bank in Cambridge was able to develop a good understanding of the banking opportunities presented by the young companies, as well as of the special problems attached to appraisal and control of them. While Bullock's original involvement had been on an informal and personal basis, nevertheless the Bank was willing to respond in support of the group by acting as its secretariat (which remains the case today), and more importantly by providing business advice and support to its members.

Barclays already occupied a special position in Cambridge. It was the longest established and largest bank in the area and also had strong connections with the University and colleges. Edmund Parker the senior local director, whose family had run the Cambridge district from Bene't Street for several generations, thus felt able to take the strategic decision to assign virtually the whole of the time of the district's business advisory services manager to the fledgling companies. He also instructed the managers at key branches to make special efforts to support the sector. After Bullock's departure in mid-1980 the crucial task of implementing and developing the business advisory service in this respect was undertaken by Walter Herriot, who is currently a manager in the Chesterton Road branch in Cambridge. Over the past five years Herriot has been involved in over 100 local high technology businesses.

Third, awareness of professional and business services firms, based locally and in London, of what was happening in Cambridge was deliberately cultivated, which laid the base for subsequent development of these sectors. That as substantial an institution as Barclays was evidently making special efforts to support the young companies helped to encourage the local firms in particular to play an active and supportive role.

Fourth, formation of the group similarly provided the basis on which meetings could be held with the local authorities. These discussions alerted the authorities to the emerging phenomenon and hence made an important contribution to development of the forward-looking planning policies that have helped the phenomenon to grow. Amongst those closely involved were Ian Purdy, then planning officer and currently director of land and buildings in the county council, and also David Urwin, the city's chief planning officer.

Finally, formation of the group gave identity and status to what was happening in Cambridge and helped it reach, more quickly than might otherwise have happened, a 'critical mass' for self-sustaining growth.

└───┘

started, and survived to emerge into a successful and prestigious firm? But in general we think that these developments, if hypothetically transferred to other possible locations one might think of, would have had some impact along the lines of what has happened in Cambridge.

5.69 There is another set of precipitating factors, some of them mentioned already though in different contexts. These factors – which have arisen for negative reasons, though usually politely referred to as 'push' factors – have been to do with the consequences of business shake-ups and failures and also of career frustrations and uncertainties. Individuals affected by such circumstances have been stimulated to set up their own businesses – such behaviour is of course not confined to Cambridge.

5.70 There are many illustrations of push factors. As can be inferred from the 'family tree' (presented in chapter 3), the break-up of Sinclair Radionics in the late 1970s, the growing difficulties of Cambridge Consultants in the late 1960s, the frustrations felt by key people in the Computer Aided Design Centre in the second half of the 1970s – in these (and other) cases there was a high level of spin-out company formation. (But by no means all spin-outs from these organisations have been prompted by such difficulties.)

5.71 In addition to such cases, numerous individual spin-outs have occurred simply because of frictions between the key personnel involved – again a not uncommon cause of new company formation. But it is the large aggregate impact of push factors in such significant cases as the three mentioned in the previous paragraph that make the matter worthy of attention.

CONCLUDING COMMENTS

5.72 In our consultations, especially once our understanding of the Cambridge scene had advanced sufficiently, we were often asked a number of general questions. These are discussed in this concluding section.

Why Cambridge and not other universities elsewhere?

5.73 This report has obviously sought to answer the first part of the question, and we believe has been able to point to a variety of factors – general and specific, historic and contemporary, technological and commercial, and so on – that taken together 'explain' the

phenomenon. To address the second part is, equally obviously, a major exercise in its own right but it is interesting to speculate a little.

5.74 It would be foolish to suggest that as other places do not have the same combination of circumstances as Cambridge, they cannot be expected to have a phenomenon of their own. After all, there is inter alia in the United States a Route 128 phenomenon and a Stanford phenomenon which, though basically similar in origin and form, have important differences. There is no necessary reason why in Britain there should be only one phenomenon, and that at Cambridge, or why the Cambridge case constitutes the only possible model for Britain.

5.75 Of course Cambridge (along with Oxford) occupies a special place in Britain, not only in higher education but also in the wider political, business and social life of the country. Of course, too, Cambridge has an unusually high concentration of academic research resources, pure and applied, in both the physical and life sciences. But Cambridge does not have a monopoly on excellence and nor does it embrace every scientific discipline with commercial application. More important, all other universities (and a good number of polytechnics) have their own substantial research groups and national or even international centres of excellence.

5.76 So why not elsewhere? At the most general level we think the answer lies, firstly, in the combination of its size and form and the role of the University in its urban environment that makes Cambridge such a special place, and where the phenomenon could be recognised as such. Secondly, it lies in the realm of the University's official policies towards commercial involvement on the part of its academics; this is so important a topic that it is returned to in its own right in a later chapter.

5.77 Beyond these levels, there will be many individual influences and constraints specific to the circumstances of each location and university, and it will be instructive to explore this a little further. It would be a nonsense to suggest we properly understand the situation at every university – that would require a study like the present one in each case. But we have had the opportunity to consider questions of industrial linkage in a good number of universities as well as the benefit of consulting several people with general and particular knowledge. What follows is thus essentially informed speculation, done most conveniently in relation to a few particular universities.

5.78 To start with, why not Oxford? It must at once be recognised that there *are* high technology firms, some of them university spin-outs, in Oxford and the surrounding villages and towns – Oxford Instruments is the best-known example, but one estimate we have been given is that there are perhaps 50 such firms in the area.

5.79 There are a number of key differences between Oxford and Cambridge Universities:

(a) Oxford has an arts:science ratio roughly of 2:1 as against 1:1 in Cambridge;

(b) Oxford has a stronger emphasis on pure science (where it too has a distinguished international reputation) as opposed to applied science – the department of engineering science (as it is called) is small and not as powerful as engineering in Cambridge which is the largest department in that university;

(c) Oxford's major scientific strength is in chemistry. There are typically very high set-up costs in the chemicals industry, which makes it a very difficult sector for small firms to enter. This may be contrasted, by way of illustration, with Cambridge's strength in computing which is so well suited to small firms;

(d) Oxford has not developed a teaching capability in microelectronics (although of course researchers in many fields use microelectronics);

(e) at risk of oversimplification, the top hierarchy in Oxford – masters of colleges, members of key committees, senior administrative officers – tends to come from and to be oriented towards the arts, government, law and politics; in Cambridge the orientation is rather more towards industry and applied science. It is instructive to note that the current three senior administrative officers of Cambridge all have doctorates in science.

5.80 Outside the universities the essential difference between Oxford and Cambridge lies in attitudes to industry and in planning policies. The motor vehicles factory at Cowley on the outskirts of Oxford has had a pervasive and negative impact. Initially the concern was that Cowley introduced an incompatible element into Oxford as a university town. More recently the decline of the UK motor industry has brought with it a new set of concerns to do with industrial unemployment and redundant industrial buildings.

5.81 Generally speaking, the net effect has been to reinforce the county council's doubts (and until recently also the University's) about the benefits of industrial development. Although the city council has for some years keenly promoted industrial development, the physical development opportunities near the University are very limited and there has been difficulty even in finding a site suitable for a science park. The consequence of all these circumstances is that new industrial development, including high technology, has had to be located in towns and larger villages within typically a 15-mile radius of the city. And this in turn has militated against formation of the networks that characterise the Cambridge phenomenon and hence too against achievement of a 'critical mass' of companies.

5.82 It is interesting also to take the case of Manchester University, and in particular to ponder why if Cambridge has experienced such a proliferation of young computer-based companies, Manchester (the other historic university centre of computing in the country – see box 5.2 earlier) has not. We suspect that, beyond the different technological orientation of the two computing departments from the outset, the reasons lie in two factors. First, the university in Manchester is effectively swamped by and 'lost' in the city as a totality. Second, and probably far more important, a close relationship existed between the computing department and a very large local company – the latter constituting the natural destination of graduates wanting to enter industry and the natural vehicle for commercial exploitation of the academics' know-how. Partly also because of the department's being very large, there has simply been less incentive for the individual academic to go out and do his own thing.

5.83 In this context it is fascinating to speculate that if IBM had been allowed to establish in Cambridge in the 1960s (see chapter 2), this might unintentionally have had an inhibiting effect on development of the local computing industry and on new company formation by individuals.

5.84 As commented earlier, these questions of scale and urban geography are probably central to explanations why there is not a concentration of small high technology companies around Imperial College in London, which is a very powerful technological university. Among some 19th-century universities – even those strong in science and technology, and not necessarily in large conurbations – the explanation probably lies rather more in the institutions having sought from the outset to be 'ivory towers', so that a culture was created which was not really conducive to academics getting involved in outside commercial activity and especially in manning their own businesses. If particular know-how has appeared suitable for exploitation, typically this has been done via licensing to an existing enterprise whether locally or beyond. In some cases – notably in the cities where shipbuilding, steel and other heavy industries were predominant – this was reinforced by the history and nature of the local business environment in which new firm formation and advanced science-based industry were the exception rather than the rule.

5.85 All these factors have been changing for several years at a quickening pace currently, and there must be few universities in which there is now no incidence of spin-out at all. But by and large, the numbers are very small and, to go on the Cambridge experience, it will take a long period of 'conditioning' for the situation to alter appreciably. (Chapter 7 discusses further these and other questions of university-industry links.)

Why has the Cambridge phenomenon taken its particular form?
5.86 Again, the basic elements to this question were addressed earlier in this chapter but it is useful to put forward a summary answer here. There are five relevant dimensions of the 'form' of the phenomenon.

5.87 First, there is its sectoral composition. The industries in which the high technology firms are concentrated reflect to an important extent the scientific and technological expertise in the University and research institutions. The high incidence of firms in, for instance, computing software (notably CAD), scientific instruments involving a variety of electron optical techniques (though the instruments sector reflects also the long history of the area's specialisation in design and manufacture of all manner of such equipment), and now increasingly firms in the biosciences, together illustrate this. The sectoral composition reflects in addition such factors as the accumulation of skill that happened to be developed over a period in Cambridge.

A good example of this would be microcomputer design where developments in the 1960s–1970s at Cambridge Consultants, PA Technology, Sinclair Radionics, various departments of the University and elsewhere, overlaid on the skill base of the Pye group and Cambridge Instruments activities, created a local capability that would be hard to match anywhere.

5.88 Second is the question of geographic location. The general preference of the firms to be in or very near Cambridge itself reflects the city's unique characteristics as well as the fact that, with most of these firms being small and not engaged in heavy production, it has been possible so far to accommodate them in a relatively small area. Also, the relative isolation of Cambridge from other large towns has meant that there has been no effective competition and this has made it the natural focal point of new activity.

5.89 The third question is to do with the type of activity. The R&D/D&D bias of the young firms in particular can be ascribed both to their 'comparative advantage' and their current stage of development. The absence of large-scale production arises from a combination of the same reasons, the local examples of Sinclair and Acorn who sub-contract volume production, and planning restrictions.

5.90 The fourth question concerns the timing of the phenomenon, why it developed when it did. The aggregate time profile of company formation and growth can be accounted for by interplay of five main developments:
   – the 1969 Mott report and the consequent evolution of physical planning policies;
   – the ripeness of particular technologies in relation to the market (eg CAD from the mid-1970s onwards, microcomputers from the late 1970s onwards, biotechnology starting in the early 1980s);
   – the fortuitously favourable timing of completion of improvements to the strategic road system;
   – the responsiveness of the local financial and business services sector in supporting the young firms in particular;
   – the cumulative demonstration effect of numerous new companies getting successfully established and making money – in some of the 'older' companies, very large amounts of money.

5.91 It is indeed extraordinary to observe that the strength of these factors (allied with the resurgence of the small firms sector nationally) has been such as to overcome the negative effects of the economic recession that has persisted, with only modest periods of improvement, since the mid-1970s.

5.92 Finally, there is the question of why there has been such a high incidence of spin-out company formation. The answer lies in:
 – the nature of the technologies and the suitability of their exploitation by small firms;
 – the individualism and high quality of the people setting up in business;
 – the 'push' factors of existing commercial employers being in trouble or of career frustrations;
 – the presence of a bank (Barclays) that was highly supportive of new technology based firms and of first-time entrepreneurs;
 – the relative lack of alternative employment for academics and others wanting to stay in the area;
 – the frustrations experienced in some instances when individuals sought to commercialise their know-how through the existing licensing channels;
 – the relative lack of existing companies available or suited to commercialise the know-how under license from the inventors, both locally (because of the limited industrial base) and beyond (because of the leading edge nature of the invention or the differences in style between the Cambridge individuals and established large companies);
 – the establishment from early on of a pattern of people leaving existing organisations to set up their own businesses;
 – the growing 'demonstration effect' afforded by the success of earlier spin-outs.

6

SOME ISSUES IN THE START-UP AND GROWTH OF SMALL HIGH TECHNOLOGY FIRMS

INTRODUCTION

6.1 This chapter is about the processes of birth and growth of small high technology companies, and the strategic issues the companies have to deal with at different stages in this development. It is based chiefly on consultations with the companies themselves and with others such as financiers and accountants in the course of this Cambridge study, supplemented by our involvement in high technology small business development programmes in other parts of the country as well as by review of literature on some of the relevant US experience (26).

6.2 In one sense the chapter is not specific to Cambridge in its applicability; one of its purposes is to help inform understanding generally of this sector because of its potential significance to the national economy in the longer term. In another sense, however, it is quite particular to Cambridge. It is framed very much with the experience of the phenomenon in mind, and it is useful as a foundation for thinking ahead (in the last chapter) about the future of the phenomenon.

6.3 There are many and sometimes major differences among small firms even in the same sector. The differences lie less in the particular products and technologies involved, and rather more in such qualitative factors as how the firms got started, the stage the firms are at in their life cycle, the goals and the perceptions of the opportunities and constraints on the part of the firms' principals, the nature of personal relationships and the overall style of the enterprise, and the like. These factors are probably all the more important in high technology firms because of the typically high proportion of well qualified and individualistic people whether principals or employees, and also because the principals are not just managers but tend to be very involved in the technology itself.

6.4 Consequently it is difficult and potentially misleading to seek to define too exactly what might constitute a 'typical' small high technology firm or even categories of firms. Nevertheless, there are a number of dimensions that are common to *all* firms: how they cope with risk, how their financing needs are met and how this changes over time, how their product mix changes, how their marketing and management systems develop, and so on. This chapter concentrates on these dimensions rather than on the firms themselves.

MODELS OF SMALL HIGH TECHNOLOGY COMPANY DEVELOPMENT

6.5 This section looks at the formation and development processes of small high technology enterprises from a number of different angles. Its purpose is to identify, within a coherent framework, the critical issues that arise in these processes.

The 'hardening' of 'soft' companies

6.6 Based on review of the experience of high technology spin-out companies from Massachusetts Institute of Technology and Stanford University, and subsequently on corresponding experience in the UK, Bullock (5, 6) has articulated a general model for the start-up and growth of such enterprises. This model provides a useful way into understanding the issues facing the development of small high technology firms generally.

6.7 The essential feature of this model is that there is a spectrum of risk, financial and technological, that faces a young high technology company. The company can get established at the low-risk end (a 'soft' start-up) and move along a development path that enables it gradually to take on bigger risks (ie to 'harden'); or it can start up anywhere along this path even, in exceptional cases, at the fully 'hard' extreme.

6.8 The typical early stages along this spectrum can be presented in simplified terms as follows:

(a) the first stage is where an academic (or equivalent) engages in outside consultancy. This typically involves applying his highly specialised knowledge to specific, one-off needs of the client (often government or a big company), and the product is an advisory report. The consultancy work is of short duration and quite compatible with the academic's remaining in the university;

(b) the next stage is for a reasonably standard analytical or design service, available on a custom-specific contract basis, to be developed out of the high-level consultancy work. Although this work will frequently prove to be the basis for a full-time commitment to the business it usually still requires only part-time involvement and hence is again compatible with retention of an academic post;

(c) this work leads naturally to identification of specific product opportunities such as a new measuring/control instrument, specialised software packages, or a special piece of hardware to 'drive' the software. This phase involves design and production of a particular product, probably on a customised basis;

(d) as in evolution of the consultancy work, the trend is to increasing standardisation of the product(s), finally reaching volume production possibly for a non-specialist market. This final stage, perhaps along with the preceding one, requires a whole-time commitment and thus the decision will invariably have been taken to give up the academic post.

6.9   At some, probably quite early point in this development process a business is formally set up. To repeat the jargon of the model, it will have had a 'soft' start and steadily changed to become fully 'hard' when it is undertaking speculative product development and production of standard goods for a large and non-specialist market. The underlying business logic of this drive to standardisation is financial: there are normally very much higher returns from a volume-produced standard item that incorporates advanced technology than from selling the technology itself on a one-off basis.

6.10   Invariably there are several individuals involved as principals at the crucial stage of entering seriously into business – a team is formed rather than an isolated individual. It is quite common in such cases for the principals to time their leaving existing employment serially in accordance with the new business's capacity to sustain a large overhead.

6.11   The minimisation of risk – the low cost of entry into business and the flexibility with which the hardening process can be managed – is central to the concept. The academic has the opportunity to acquire substantial business experience and to test the water without fear of sacrificing his career or even of losing money, before deciding to plunge fully into commercial life. Start-up cash flow problems are minimised, and probably do not even arise. While initially the income generated is probably marginal, it can be developed to a point where leaving present employment and covering the full costs of launching a new business can be safely achieved. The muddle-through periods that soft-starts typically experience can be reasonably well accommodated, allowing time for learning and for conflicting goals to be clarified and resolved. Knowledge of the market is empirically based and the pace of hardening can be varied accordingly. The hardening process can even be halted or reversed if necessary, and the activity might continue in high-level bespoke con-

sultancy only. At the other extreme intermediate stages can be jumped and a hard company put into operation very quickly.

6.12   There are several variants to this basic model. For instance, the company founder need not be an academic but could be in any other kind of employment; in this case he 'moonlights' in order to get his new business going or, more exceptionally, he is explicitly encouraged and helped to spin out by his existing employer. Similarly, consultancy and contract research are not the only ways into generating early cash flow or acquiring new business experience – dealerships are an example of a not uncommon alternative and indeed, though perhaps riskier, are probably a quicker way of generating cash flow. In some cases – CIS in Cambridge would be a good example – a hardware distributorship is combined with development of bespoke software for use with the hardware, so that cash is raised from both sources.

6.13   The American experience demonstrates the wide variety of approaches taken along the soft-hard spectrum, with a growing trend to skipping the early stages and becoming fully hard more quickly. This is due to the 'recycling' of technological entrepreneurs as they spin out to start again from the large companies that had acquired their first venture, as well as to the growing ability of the financial and business services community to understand and support young advanced technology enterprises.

6.14   This soft-hard model provides a very useful way of looking at the business development problems of firms in the Cambridge phenomenon. There have been classically soft starts, both from the University and from other 'sheltered' environments (such as some from the Computer Aided Design Centre in the period 1977–1983), as some of the company profiles given in chapters 3 and 4 demonstrate. Other profiles show how some companies have quickly (and successfully) become hard. Of course, not all new starts have had the 'luxury' of a planned and steady entry into business: a company formed under pressure of its parent's failure has invariably had to generate cash flow quickly; but the hardening concept still remains valid.

6.15   In terms of the model, the Cambridge phenomenon is so far made up mostly of companies at the softer end of the spectrum. The pure soft start is in abundant evidence in the University and elsewhere. Also, a high proportion of the existing company population is concentrated on research-design-development activity, and in those few cases where large-scale production has followed it is handled on a sub-contract basis by low cost plants elsewhere in the country or abroad. There are even a few Cambridge companies that have 'softened', ie they have pulled back into consultancy or R&D/D&D after having previously been hard. But there are signs of a modest degree of hardening, particularly as business experience and confidence grow and individuals by-pass or at least greatly telescope the early purely soft stages.

Financing of small high technology companies

6.16 A key feature of the soft company model is that it shows the importance of early revenues generated by consultancy or other, probable part-time activity. This approach serves to minimise cash flow problems that typically bedevil young companies and possibly also to build up a cash reserve to help later stage development. It is useful to pursue this line of thinking in a more general way and look at the financing needs of the companies especially at their initial stage of development.

6.17 The following three basic start-up financing models have applied in Cambridge:

(a) soft starts roughly as above, with the founders continuing to hold their academic positions or other jobs, including those in other high technology companies in which moonlighting is possible. In the latter cases, the host organisation may provide general support or even directly practical assistance including finance to the would-be spin-outs. (Cambridge Consultants set up a business division specifically for this purpose, which has itself recently spun out as an enterprise in its own right.) For the new start, internal cash generation is typically sufficient to make external funding unnecessary;

(b) also soft starts, but the founders set up full-time in business at once, initially undertaking a variety of activities (such as consultancy, dealerships or other agency functions), that are not central to longer-term development of their businesses. But these activities, perhaps augmented by an overdraft facility, generate sufficient cash to permit development work on the products they really are interested in to proceed simultaneously. In some cases these initial activities are dropped as soon as possible; in others they are con-

tinued, albeit at a lower level and probably as incidental to their core business;

(c) the company founders have a product idea, more or less well researched, which needs further design and development (maybe research too) on an intensive and full-time basis. They are able to put up some money themselves but additional finance from external sources is usually essential. The development period and the capital required can vary greatly, from short and minimal (a couple of months and zero respectively, at one extreme) in the case of software products to long and substantial (several years and up to say £1 million respectively, at the other) in the case of biotechnology.

6.18 It is instructive to discuss the main sources of finance for these different kinds of ventures.

6.19 Overdraft facilities made available by the clearing banks constitute a principal source of start-up finance for companies that do not have sizeable fixed capital requirements. (They typically remain an element in longer-term financing, alongside term borrowing or other fixed capital, for regular working capital purposes.) Practice among the clearing banks varies, but it has become increasingly common for the amount of the facility to be set in relation to the value of debtors and for use of the facility to be monitored in relation to other agreed indicators of company performance.

6.20 Term finance (often backed by the government's loan guarantee scheme for small firms) is commonly used by the clearing banks in start-up ventures with lead times for product development of say up to one year. The finance is usually structured in relation to an agreed business plan, and successive tranches of funds automatically released only if the development programme (in terms of money and time) is being adhered to. (Because of this feature, overdraft and term facilities may not be strictly distinguishable.) As noted in earlier chapters, a fundamental feature of Barclays' lending to young high technology enterprises in Cambridge has been imposition of management discipline by means of intensive monitoring of this kind.

6.21 The nature of the bulk of the Cambridge phenomenon companies up to now is such that their start-up and early financing has been well suited to support from the clearing banks along the above lines. This partly explains the dominance to date of Barclays as a source of funds.

6.22 Term finance provided for start-up purposes by a clearing bank has so far typically gone up to a maximum of £75 000, which is the upper limit of the small firms loan guarantee scheme. This has proved sufficient for the bulk of the soft start-up firms. However, if larger sums have been required – invariably the case for ventures starting at once with 'hard' products, or for development projects with high equipment costs or with very long lead times as in biotechnology – then several principal sources of funds have been available. These have included special 'windows' set up by the clearing banks, financial institutions such as ICFC and NRDC, ad hoc consortia of institutional interests (nowadays with a few of the Cambridge colleges among them), venture capital firms and a variety of approaches that might include wealthy local individuals or use of funds established under the government's business expansion scheme. In terms of the maturing of the phenomenon it is important to understand that, with the main exceptions of ICFC and NRDC, these sources of capital have not really been involved in the phenomenon until the last few years.

6.23 Of these sources the venture capital group is of particular interest because of its very recent establishment in Britain. There are now approximately 100 private sector funds in Britain that describe themselves as providing venture capital. But probably fewer than a dozen of them are seriously interested in start-up high technology ventures. Those that are interested are typically run by a very small group of businessmen who have international financial and marketing experience, and often a spell in the US venture capital industry; they are willing, and expect, to commit substantial amounts of their own time to helping the enterprises they support through the critical start-up and formative phases.

6.24 Because of the labour-intensity of such work, there is a real limit to the number of start-up or very young firms that these venture funds can take into their portfolios, due to constraints on the managers' time plus the need to have a portfolio of balanced maturity. The consequence is that the funds feel compelled not to take on too many small projects and seldom if ever find it worthwhile to make investments of less than about £200 000; indeed the current trend among the better established funds is for this lower limit to rise to £500 000 or even £750 000.

6.25 There is thus a gap between what term finance and clearing banks will readily provide (say £75 000) and the minimum point at which a venture capital firm will make an investment (say £200 000). This gap has so far been successfully filled by the other sources of finance noted in paragraph 6.22, though it is worth observing that in some of the cases the assembly of a suitable financing package can become a complicated and time-consuming affair.

6.26 One of the distinctive features of the start-up financing we have been describing is the close relationship that develops in some (but not all) cases between the firm and the financier. The latter will be watching two particular aspects of the business: satisfactory execution of the R&D/D&D programme as explained earlier and, in the next phase, the build-up of sales. Over-optimism on one or other or even both these counts – under-estimating the development time and costs and over-estimating the rate of growth of sales – stands out as the most important cause of the business failures experienced so far.

6.27 Once successfully launched, those Cambridge companies that have remained at the soft end of the spectrum have typically had few problems in generating enough funds internally to make a substantial if not total contribution to the financing of their own development. Expansion has invariably required a greater working capital facility from their banks, but this has seldom been a problem.

6.28 By contrast, as one would expect, companies at the harder end of the spectrum or those that are hardening rapidly have generally needed second and subsequent rounds of external finance for particular investment projects. The longer established or more successful the firm, naturally the easier it has been to raise money from one or more of the several sources mentioned above; it has in fact become easier to do so in the past one or two years. Sometimes a restraint on mobilising external funds can be imposed by the firm itself in that its founders are unwilling to give up equity. Our impression is that this well-known attitude of British small firms is held rather less strongly in Cambridge than elsewhere (though it is still encountered, especially at the start-up stage). This is because there is a realistic appreciation both of the benefits of equity finance in situations of rapid growth and of the value of offering equity to key individuals joining or being promoted in the firm after its initial capitalisation.

6.29 Second and later round financing differs from that at start-up in a few main respects. A track record is building up so the risks are easier to assess, and it will be easier for financiers to justify the probably much larger sums required. There are several more sources of finance open to the borrower. In addition to government schemes for promoting innovation and the private sector institutions, both discussed earlier, these sources include the new venture management funds now becoming active in Cambridge. There are also the unlisted securities market (USM) and ultimately the stock exchange, though these may represent the 'end of the road' rather more than an intermediate financing stage. The USM exercises a particular attraction to the young and more ambitious company founders, as it is seen as something that is realistic to aim for in a fairly short time and that will be financially very rewarding to them as individuals.

6.30 There is a final key difference between start-up and later financing. This is that at certain critical stages in a firm's development the latter may coincide with a need for additional and different marketing and management resources (sometimes more pressing than the need for extra financial resources). This is well illustrated by the experience of a couple of the firms that have sold out to large US firms precisely to secure a combination of these resources that could not be satisfactorily obtained piecemeal in Britain. This is thus an appropriate point to turn to the marketing, management and related aspects of small high technology companies' development.

6.31 Before doing so, however, it is worth repeating the broad conclusion that shortage of capital is not a limiting factor in Cambridge on the start-up and development of the firms. Further, the availability of capital has undoubtedly been much more than simply constituting a negative factor. It has itself encouraged people to take risks and brought more deals to the market: in this sense it has been an important positive stimulus too. The ready availability of debt finance from the clearing bank sector starting in the late 1970s has thus exercised a profoundly important long-term multiplier effect on the quantity and quality of investment capital accessible to Cambridge companies.

Marketing, management and organisational development

6.32 No matter how brilliant the original idea or even how successfully executed, the chances are that the business abilities of a young high technology firm start being fully tested only at later stages of its development. The banks and other investors experienced in financing such companies are keenly aware of this: there is usually no less concern about the qualities of the management team than about the technology, and about the ability to generate a future stream of sound products than about the outstanding qualities of the first product in particular.

6.33 It is not hard to see why this should be so, and it is most simply shown by drawing a somewhat exaggerated caricature of a Cambridge start-up company:

(a) the founders – as already observed, there are usually (and beneficially) more than one – see a market niche or else believe they have a technology that could be so developed as to create demand. Either way they are likely to be more interested and capable in respect of the technology per se than the market. They are referred to as technology-driven; for survival and growth they will need to become market-led;

(b) their first sales come from exploiting an informal network of contacts on which the principals have credibility and perhaps goodwill. This may be local or further afield (exceptionally abroad). In a few cases an absence of a formal marketing effort can prevail indefinitely – mostly not. Marketing skills must be developed or bought-in;

(c) the pressures to move into export markets sooner rather than later can be intense. It is commonly said that the UK represents perhaps no more than 5% of the market for high technology goods (obviously with sectoral variations). So marketing, distribution and after-sales servicing arrangements will have to be decided and put in place. Should the company take on the full executive responsibilities itself (unrealistic for the bulk of small companies) or should it establish an agency arrangement? In the latter event how is the agent selected? – it seems that too often in the past it has been the foreign agent who has selected the Cambridge company. And are favourable terms negotiated (notably including those governing control of the intellectual property rights)?;

(d) the firm starts off with one product idea or perhaps a set of related ideas. The firm's competitive edge is likely to lie in its technology; so a continuing

R&D/D&D programme must be sustained, perhaps moving into new fields, at the same time as marketing and other strategic functions are being developed;

(e) the firm almost certainly starts off with a very informal organisational structure and style. This suits the individualistic style typical of Cambridge. Those that have spun directly out of the University or other research groups have often carried an academic 'lifestyle' with them. At some point a strategic choice must be made as to whether or not the firm wants (or needs) to grow, and the consequences of growth accepted as it impinges on its nature and style. Yet, R&D and D&D activity especially in the sectors in which Cambridge is specialised is invariably most fruitfully performed in an informal environment. So, how is informality and intellectual fertility maintained in a (fast) growing organisation that probably has to become more structured?;

(f) as a company hardens can it develop the requisite production engineering and management skills?; or if it sub-contracts volume production, can it ensure the maintenance of quality and also properly control the long supply lines frequently involved?

6.34 There are two deliberate omissions from the above. First, there is no reference to what might be described as routine management skills involving timely generation of vital management accounting information. This is not because they are irrelevant – lack of real knowledge of what is going on in the business is an endemic problem for soft companies and also for those that are growing extremely fast. Nor is it because they cease to increase in complexity as the firm's operations extend into new product, market and currency areas. Rather it is because, as the local banking and business community will testify, the firm's principals are usually fairly easily able to acquire these skills (perhaps writing their own management accounting software) even if they have no prior business experience. Nevertheless, it would be misleading to play down entirely these issues of routine management information – all too often the systems are set up late, and there have been a few extreme cases in which such weaknesses have been a principal cause of business failure.

6.35 Second, there is no question of the basic motivation and ambitions of the great bulk of the companies. A decade or so ago there probably generally prevailed an experimental or lifestyle approach. This cannot be said to be the case now. The combination of local

examples of success which have resulted in individuals not unlike themselves becoming very well off, the growing social acceptance and status of being in high technology industry and the strong outside interest shown in individual companies, has resulted generally in the firms recognising that being in business is a serious matter and also that making money is a highly desirable reward for all the effort put into achieving success.

6.36 The issues raised in paragraph 6.33 concerning the growth of young high technology firms can be summed up:

(a) a balanced management team must be built up, that introduces the requisite marketing, personnel management, negotiating and other hard business skills to complement the initial technological skills;

(b) the organisation must grow and its structure develop so that the essential business disciplines are introduced without simultaneously de-motivating the staff and inhibiting their innovativeness.

6.37 Clearly there is no single way of addressing these issues that satisfies all firms. Hence each firm must find its own best solutions. But a few broadly applicable comments can be made.

6.38 First, the critical requirement in the early stages of development is assembly of the right team of key individuals. It is these individuals who must set corporate strategy across the whole spectrum of operations and around whom the organisational structure must evolve. The emphasis that the financial sector increasingly places on formation of such a team is indicative of the weight of the matter; indeed some financing bodies will themselves concentrate their attention on putting a team together if they believe the venture is basically worth backing but the principals lack the requisite skills.

6.39 Building such a team is far from easy, especially if new management skills are to be introduced in good time for the next stage of the company's development. For instance, tricky problems face a young or small technology-driven firm that is committed to developing its export trade. One option is to seek to recruit an international marketing specialist. But this is not so straightforward: such a person can command a very high salary (even with the favourable changes recently introduced in the share options legislation), which can mean uncomfortable salary differentials and even cash flow problems; recruitment costs can be very high too; the search for the right person can take many months even with the help of recruitment consultants.

6.40 Another option is to cope without a highly qualified marketing executive. So far because of their leading market positions many of even the more mature Cambridge firms have not found it necessary to have such a post. Instead they have worked through foreign firms acting in an agency capacity, often after the latter themselves have taken the initiative to play this role. In some cases these marketing-cum-distribution systems have worked exceptionally well and led to close inter-company relationships. But in general we doubt that the Cambridge firms will be able to afford not to give strategic coherence to their marketing and to take initiatives themselves, and so bringing in the right skill for this purpose, perhaps initially on a part-time basis, will be essential.

6.41 A third option is to use outside experts on a consultancy basis. This is increasingly emerging – whether in marketing or other areas of strategic management support – as a practicable approach, that probably could not even have been anticipated say only five or even two years ago. The reason is that as the phenomenon has become publicised so has it 'sucked in' individuals (often themselves Cambridge graduates) with substantial and specialised business experience who see the opportunity to add value in particular ways to the young Cambridge firms.

6.42 By way of example, a Cambridge-trained CAD expert has returned to Cambridge after several years of experience in Japan, to set up a firm offering consultancy services not so much in CAD as in trade with Far Eastern countries. There are equivalent examples in other management fields. In general we think these small, specialised consultancy firms, along with the new venture management firms discussed elsewhere, stand an excellent chance of successfully supporting the young high technology firms because of a basically shared style and approach to business.

6.43 A second issue of business development concerns organisational change. Growth of a firm necessarily implies increasing complexity of its management functions and hence a rising need for some formalisation of responsibilities. Two or three founders can cover the whole range of activities together probably without formal allocation of tasks. By the time there are say 8–10 employees, several being highly qualified, depending on the exact nature of the businesses the chances are that they will need to be broken into two smaller units organised on a project basis.

6.44 As growth proceeds, the need remains to keep small project teams whose composition will vary from one project to another; alternatively specialist divisions may be formed. Deployment and motivation of staff thus becomes increasingly important. In addition, corporate planning and management as well as routine business administration become progressively more time-consuming. When a firm reaches say 25–30 staff there is usually a need for a properly defined (though not rigid) corporate structure in which the roles of at least the managing, research, technical, finance and marketing directors are reasonably defined. A proper personnel policy starts becoming more important too, perhaps including formulae for participation in the profits or equity of the business.

6.45 Further growth will induce further organisational adjustments; though what the appropriate structure is can only be judged on an individual basis depending on the nature of the firm's products and activities, its geographic scope and so on. Nevertheless, continuing organisational development must be expected; certainly faster growth will mean faster obsolescence of existing structures and more frequent need for new ones. Management of such a potentially 'unstable' system becomes a skill of the highest order, again especially if it is to be deployed in good time rather than have continuously to be 'fire-fighting'. Those so far relatively few Cambridge firms that have grown rapidly beyond 50–100 employees have shown a high degree of strategic management skill.

6.46 A third business development issue is that while growth beyond a certain point is undoubtedly necessary for survival, beyond a further point it may become counter-productive. The firm can become so large that the communications, formal and informal, break down or at least cease to take place spontaneously, with the consequence that the vitality, on which success was initially based, begins to wane.

6.47 It is striking how many Cambridge firms seem to have recognised this. They have stabilised their total size at anywhere between say 50 and 200 employees which in their particular products and technologies they judge to be optimal, in the sense of achieving the necessary economies of scale and none of the diseconomies. We suspect in any event that the Cambridge management style, if one can seek to generalise, is at its best in organisations that do not get too big.

6.48 This is at variance with the American experience. It seems to be a particular American skill to be able to mobilise all the requisite resources to grow a new technology enterprise into an enormous, fully integrated company in a short time – witness Wang, Hewlett Packard, Digital, Control Data and the like. In their different ways the Japanese and the Germans have this same skill too. By contrast, it has long been the Cambridge skill to produce an abundance of new ideas and it is now also its skill to exploit them commercially though not, so far, on a large scale.

CONCLUDING COMMENTS

6.49 This chapter has sought to comment on the general business development issues facing small high technology firms in general and in Cambridge in particular. Little of it will be new to the companies themselves. We were struck by how aware they typically are of what the issues and options are. Their difficulties lie rather in actually taking the right strategic decisions and in having the managerial experience and strength to push things through effectively.

6.50 There is no substitute for learning by doing in respect of these management matters. The growing presence on the Cambridge business network of individuals with specialised business experience and of business consultancy firms will hasten this process. There are already also a number of cases in which recently retired company directors of wide experience are working closely with young companies. The 're-cycling' of the technological entrepreneurs themselves, each time with additional experience, will also make a significant contribution; so will the increased strength and sophistication of the financial and business services community.

6.51 There are thus solid grounds for optimism about the ability of the young companies to increase their management and business strength. This is one of numerous reasons for our being bullish about the prospects of the phenomenon (see chapter 8).

6.52 This confidence does not gainsay the inevitable problems of growth that the young firms will have to go through. Not all of them will be able to mobilise the marketing, management and other resources needed to sustain and complement their technological excellence. Pressures for rationalisation and consolidation of very small and highly specialised firms will undoubtedly grow.

6.53 How such changes might be effected is returned to in chapter 8. No further comment is needed here except to observe that the spectrum of business development issues raised by the Cambridge high technology firms is of far more than local interest. It may be that the issues are more readily discernible in Cambridge because of the sheer volume of companies there, but they are of much wider applicability and are collectively a matter of national concern. Cambridge-style new technology based firms have potentially a major role to play in the national economy; and the Cambridge experience provides an invaluable learning ground of leading-edge experience, in terms of business as well as technology.

7

UNIVERSITY-INDUSTRY LINKS: SOME LESSONS
FROM THE CAMBRIDGE EXPERIENCE

INTRODUCTION

7.1   There have over the past few decades been various waves of enthusiasm for improving the linkages between, on the one hand, higher educational and research institutions as generators of know-how and, on the other, business and industry and government bodies as users of know-how. (For short-hand, we use 'universities' to denote the former category and 'industry' the latter.) Previous waves have tended to subside leaving behind few enduring structures as well as a sense of dissatisfaction that an unharnessed potential remained that nobody could quite see how to tackle. The wave of interest over the past two–three years promises to be something different, if only because the universities are under great financial pressure and feel they have a real incentive to do something effective.

7.2   The consequence is that many new initiatives are being taken on campuses up and down the country. Those typically comprise science parks and related schemes, strengthening and diversification of existing industrial liaison arrangements or establishment of new ones, and in general a good deal of experimentation in cultivating links of all kinds with industry. The frequency of press articles and of conferences testify to the large number of initiatives and the huge interest in this field.

7.3   We have had occasion in other contexts to work directly in, or become acquainted at first-hand with, over 30 higher educational institutions specifically in respect of their industrial linkage policies and mechanisms. This experience makes us cautious to seek to generalise too readily about the deficiencies or otherwise and the long-term outcome of what is currently under way in university-industry matters, for seven principal reasons.

7.4   First, there are enormous differences among universities in their size, mix of disciplines and technological strength. At one extreme Cambridge is a large and well-resourced university by UK standards, with a powerful technological capability. At the other extreme are some of the small new universities either with an orientation to the arts and social sciences or, if technologically based, probably severely constrained for staff and other resources. Clearly there are likely to be different capabilities in respect of industrial links among the different institutions.

7.5   Second, not all universities have exactly the same objectives, or balance among several objectives, in respect of their links with industry. For instance, those that are concerned primarily to raise revenue from commercialisation of their know-how are led into rather different policies compared with those whose basic motivation is to ensure the relevance and up-to-dateness of their teaching and research.

7.6   Third, the institutions vary enormously among themselves in their experience and perceptions of industry and in their organisational structure and style. These differences reflect a mix of each institution's origins and local economic environment, subsequent accidents of history, the impact of powerful individuals and, at any one time, the interplay of senior personalities in the administration and the faculties. The capacity of the institutions, qua institutions, to get involved in industrial liaison varies accordingly.

7.7   Fourth, it is not always easy to discern exactly what a university's policies are towards industrial links or what actually is taking place, whether because or despite of these policies. This can apply even where a university apparently has articulated its policies and/or has a formal industrial liaison mechanism in place. There are too many factors, not all of them amenable to orderly central management, that bear upon industrial linkages, and typically also too much happening for everything about a university's industrial liaison system to be the same in actuality as might be supposed at first sight.

7.8   Fifth, as noted earlier, practice varies among universities in the contractual arrangements with their staff. A few (of which Cambridge is one) have terms of service that are very loosely specified and give a great deal of freedom to the individual. But the majority have more tightly drawn contracts which in principle limit the individual's freedom to engage in outside work; though the actual extent of such limitation differs from one institution to another depending on how rigorously the formal contractual obligations are enforced.

7.9   Sixth, there is not a single way of doing things. A recent study of university-industry relations in the USA (27) has identified a huge number (literally hundreds) of different kinds of links. Even within the same broad category, many significant variants are possible. This last point can be illustrated with reference to a science park.

7.10 The concept of a university science park is essentially very simple. There is no special theory that underpins its design or operation, and equally no magic that makes one successful. No two science parks should expect to be the same because of differences in their academic, market, financial and physical circumstances, and in the personalities involved. Consequently, while the experience that is now steadily accumulating is facilitating identification of what constitutes best practice in different circumstances, there is no basis for unqualified prescriptions as to the do's and don'ts of science parks in general. The same applies to other areas of university-industry relationships.

7.11 Seventh, the gestation periods before individual schemes start making a real impact are long – witness the experience of the Cambridge science park which, even in highly favourable local circumstances, has taken all of a decade to grow to a substantial size. Also, the roles played by schemes can change over time. On the one hand, what initially promises to be helpful can turn out to be an obstacle or a source of frustration; on the other, even if the original expectations are not fulfilled the eventual outcome can still be favourable – witness the history of the Computer Aided Design Centre and, despite its problems, the significant contribution it has made directly and indirectly to the Cambridge phenomenon. In these respects, it is early days yet to express judgment on the recent developments in the university-industry scene in Britain today.

7.12 These seven qualifications having been expressed, however, the Cambridge experience is so unusual in Britain and raises such fundamental issues for academic-industry liaison generally that it is appropriate to reflect on what lessons can be learned from Cambridge that might usefully apply elsewhere. The Cambridge experience is particularly helpful in illuminating some of the key issues in the university-industry scene, viz ownership of intellectual property rights (which will become all the more important as the statutory first rights of the British Technology Group are removed) and risk/liability considerations.

7.13 Two final caveats. This chapter is not uncritically about setting up Cambridge as a model that is appropriate everywhere else. And it pays attention to only some of the factors – albeit very important ones – that influence the total university-industry scene in any particular location. These wider considerations were discussed in chapter 5 in addressing the question as to why there was a Cambridge phenomenon but not (yet) an equivalent phenomenon elsewhere in Britain.

INTELLECTUAL PROPERTY RIGHTS, RISK AND LIABILITY, AND INDUSTRIAL LIAISON

7.14 A singular feature of the Cambridge phenomenon is that Cambridge University is one of the very few British universities that have, for conscious and positive reasons, avoided a structured and detailed policy governing links with industry. The University's position, consistent with the principles of academic freedom, as it has evolved to date can be simply stated in five points.

7.15 First, ownership of intellectual property vests with the individuals concerned unless the contract governing the work in which the know-how is acquired specifies otherwise. The University expressly eschews any control over or financial interest in exploitation of an academic's know-how, except where the academic himself asks the University to play such a role; the relative roles of the different parties are then determined by negotiation.

7.16 The underlying premise is that it is for the individual academic to decide whether or not to exploit his know-how commercially. It will be on his motivation and skill that successful exploitation must ultimately depend; the University cannot substitute for these attributes, nor can it exercise any compulsion. Similarly, in those cases where exploitation involves taking out patents and potentially other expensive actions, the University does not have the resources to take on a primary role, and it is unlikely to be properly equipped to develop patentable ideas.

7.17 If exploitation of an individual's know-how acquired in the course of his academic work were to yield very substantial profits – as might happen exceedingly infrequently in the case of an invention – then the University might seek to become involved in some way in order to acquire a proportion of that profit. Ideally this would happen through the individuals concerned voluntarily assigning a share to the University – there are precedents, notably in the United States, for endowments of this kind.

7.18 Second, the University has correspondingly always taken a relaxed and liberal attitude towards faculty members' spending time on outside work; the loose definition of the terms of service of staff makes no provision in this respect whatsoever. The natural presumption is that (in most even if not all disciplines) anybody who is any good will automatically be engaged in consulting or other outside activities; and that this is beneficial for their 'inside' work too.

7.19 The University authorities realistically recognise that it is impossible for them to know about and to exercise any effective control over how individual staff members spend their time. The institution is far too large, complex and in effect fragmented for such a centralised approach to be feasible even if it were desirable. The autonomy of the colleges – together with the teaching and other duties exercised in them by University staff members who are also college fellows, which 'cut across' their departmental responsibilities – underlines the impossibility of a monolithic approach.

7.20 In the view of the University, three sanctions are available to control the extent of outside involvements: student pressure and peer group pressure (perhaps ultimately expressed through a head of department) if an individual is quite evidently neglecting his agreed teaching or research duties, and the sense of responsibility on the part of the concerned individual himself. The University is conscious that such vague sanctions can be broken, as is known to happen in the those universities in the United States where liberal regimes apply, but believes that it happens exceedingly seldom and that it is a small price to pay for the wider freedoms its policies allow.

7.21 Third, as a necessary converse of the above policies the University has never accepted that it has any legal liability for work done by faculty members for outside bodies. If the rewards accrue to the academics, the latter must accept the risks too and make their own arrangements for doing so by forming limited liability companies and/or taking out indemnity insurance or in whatever way may be appropriate.

7.22 This, like patent and intellectual property law, is recognised as a complex issue. What happens, for instance, if an academic undertakes an external consultancy in his personal capacity but, whether intentionally or otherwise, conducts the contractual and other correspondence on officially headed departmental notepaper? Nevertheless, nobody has ever challenged the University's policy of disclaiming liability, and the policy appears to be well understood by academics.

7.23 Fourth, the University believes that in a business sense, as well as ethically from the point of view of accountability for public expenditure, its practice of charging fully for the use of its facilities in private consultancies or commercial development of know-how, is both proper and sufficient.

7.24 Fifth, in line with the above philosophy, the concept of the industrial liaison function is that it is to provide a window through which the outside world can look into the University, as well as an enabling mechanism for contacts to be made. There is no compulsion on anybody inside or outside to work through this system. The industrial liaison function is carried out by the Wolfson Cambridge Industrial Unit, which has recently been revamped to embrace the whole University (having earlier covered only the engineering department) in response to growing complaints from outside industry as to how difficult it was to know how to approach the University on specialist topics.

7.25 An interesting new development is that by which the University, while maintaining its 'laid-back' posture, recognises that there are some academics who need help in getting to exploit their know-how effectively. This could involve advice or assistance in patenting and licensing, business plan formulation, introducing prospective sources of finance or whatever else may be appropriate to the circumstances. The Wolfson Unit is now starting to provide this service, and any strengthening of its capability will be taken strictly in line with demand and in a way that will allow the University to maintain a position of not accepting liability.

7.26 In those few cases that have arisen to date where academics have asked the University to handle commercial development of their ideas, the University uses the device of a limited liability company at arm's length from itself. This company, which has the arbitrary name of Lynxvale, was originally set up to deal with the business side of a University museum. In the past year or two this company has started to generate quite handsome profits, which are covenanted to the University, from the licensing-out of several inventions made by faculty members. At present Cambridge is making a great deal more money out of industrial liaison than it puts in, which must surely be exceptional in the higher educational sector in the country.

7.27 The above discussion may be summed up by saying that, based on an accumulation of history but also as a deliberate strategic choice, the University has a benign and gently supportive posture towards faculty members' involvements of all kinds with industry. It is perfectly in order for individuals to engage in outside work on their own account if they want to, and perfectly in order if they do not.

7.28 This permissive approach has had two effects of great consequence (which were mentioned in chapter 5 but need repeating here). First, it has made it easy for academics to enter into commercial activity and to move increasingly in this direction if they wish while still maintaining their academic posts and salaries. In the case of those (relatively few) who have moved fully into business life and remained in Cambridge, the ease and acceptance of the transition have readily allowed undisturbed retention of professional and social links with former departments and colleagues. In general, the risks to income and lifestyle associated with the transition have been minimised.

7.29 Second, the liberal policies have helped create a relaxed and generous attitude on the part of individual faculty members and departments in their dealings with the outside business world. Where the businesses are small high technology firms in Cambridge itself, this attitude – reinforced by the compactness of Cambridge as a community, the abundance of social and business networks that so often originate and inter-connect in the colleges, the informality of academic-industry dealings and the calibre of people involved – has in turn allowed the individuals or departments concerned to play both a stimulating and a supportive role in development of the young firms. These considerations apply even where neither founders nor employees of the firms are Cambridge graduates, though the familiarity of the latter with 'the system' obviously facilitates the process of technology transfer. There are numerous examples and a long history of such positive relationships between local companies and the academic community (going back to the early days of Cambridge Instruments and Pye in the last century); and there is no doubt that a less liberal policy towards industrial links would have inhibited even if not actually prevented development of these relationships.

7.30 These two consequences – along with many other factors, some of them more directly influential, as discussed in earlier chapters – have in turn underpinned the growth in the Cambridge area of a thriving community of small, high technology firms. In this respect, it is a quite distinctive feature of Cambridge University's links with industry that where these are most evidently flourishing is with locally based small firms. This contrasts with the pattern at most other universities where links are typically strongest with large, probably non-local firms. (Cambridge has these latter kinds of links too; though it is our impression that, especially given the University's size and status, they are not markedly stronger in number and quality than those of other universities elsewhere.)

7.31 In sum, the fundamental feature of Cambridge's policy towards links with industry in the context of the phenomenon is this. The University's consciously relaxed attitude and the simplicity of its industrial liaison arrangements have together helped nurture a 'culture' that encourages and is supportive of links with industry. They are based on a confidence that research excellence will find potential commercial application; and, rather differently, also on a realistic appreciation both of what a central authority can achieve (especially in an old and large collegiate university) and of the primary role that must be played by the individual academic if his know-how is to be commercialised.

7.32 In effect, therefore, the thinking that underlay formation of the Mott committee has been translated into a central element in the University's policies towards many aspects of its development and its posture towards the outside world. An environment – rather than a specific instrument – for industrial linkage has been created, that is both fertile and in tune with the University's strategic interest and style.

7.33 It is perhaps in these respects that the Cambridge approach stands in sharpest contrast to those of most other British universities: a central perception of the strategic value of industrial links and a commitment to its realisation, and to do so through reliance on research excellence and on liberal ground-rules governing its exploitation rather than by means of formal regulation and institutional devices.

7.34 Generalisations about industrial linkage policies among British universities are not easy, for the reasons given at the start of this chapter, but a few observations can be made. Universities can in this context be placed into two broad categories. The first category comprises those that have not been greatly concerned, at least up to now, about links with industry. They have set up no formal arrangements and by default there probably exists a liberal regime regarding the rewards and risks of commercialisation. But the culture of the university is likely to be inimical to industrial application, and the absence of rules is not sufficient to enable links to develop and flourish.

7.35 In the second category there are those that take industrial liaison more or less seriously and have set up special mechanisms to promote it. There are essentially three ways in which the industrial liaison function is exercised.

7.36 The first way is through appointment of an industrial liaison officer, located within the administration. This arrangement can suffer from the defect that it is subject to the workings of the academic bureaucracy and consequently cannot be operated with the flexibility and speed that outside business dealings demand. Also if he is not accorded very senior status, the officer is unlikely to be particularly effective in his dealings *inside* the university, and industrial liaison considerations may not become an integral element in the university's strategic thinking and attitudes to the outside world. But these deficiencies do not always arise; Heriot-Watt stands as an interesting example among those universities where the industrial liaison function is constituted along these lines and works well.

7.37 The second way involves setting up the industrial liaison function as a limited liability company at arm's length from the university; this arrangement seems currently to be regaining favour after having been widely rejected in the 1970s. In some cases, the company builds up its own contract research staff in order to overcome the problems created by the limited and unpredictable availability of regular academic staff for large-scale outside work; this tends to result in much of the company's work and interest actually growing away from the university.

7.38 Within this approach there is a recent trend towards establishing subsidiary companies in individual specialist departments or based on particular projects. The industrial liaison company itself becomes in effect a sort of holding company. Because of the involvement of different outside parties in these different ventures, or because of the difficulty of achieving a clear demarcation of what is properly a university matter and what commercial business, the arrangements can get quite complicated. Also, there is a tendency for the university to want to exercise control over at least the holding company's affairs, especially if its own name is explicitly in the name of the latter. For these reasons the potential advantages of an arm's length company are not always realised, and also the university can get drawn into commercial matters which it is not particularly well equipped to handle.

7.39 The third way is where a variety of initiatives are taken and institutional mechanisms set up, reflecting the wide scope that exists for industrial liaison activities. Provision of continuing education, joint university-industry sponsorship, integrated chairs on the German model, involvement of industrialists in setting a university's research programme, establishment of specialist applied research institutes – these are among the many kinds of initiative that are taken. Some universities (of which Salford is rightly known as an outstanding example) have a deliberately planned and successful mix of such activities.

7.40 In the second and third approaches discussed above, there is a noticeable though not universal tendency for the university authorities to seek to want to know everything that is going on by way of external links and to control or at least to influence as much of it as possible. One of the direct consequences of this is that a good number of academics are driven 'underground' in undertaking their outside work to avoid what they see as unnecessary and obstructive bureaucratic impositions. There are universities where, despite and because of a strong central line on industrial links, probably more than 50% of outside consultancies are done 'covertly'.

7.41 Interestingly, it is our observation that the precise form of institutional arrangement matters rather less to the success of industrial linkage activity than does the history of the institution's relationship with industry and the authority's overall policy towards new relationships. Thus those universities that have grown out of colleges of advanced technology or similar institutes, or those that have long specialised in applied science and engineering, tend to have a rich diversity of industrial links irrespective of how they structure their industrial liaison arrangements.

7.42 A facet of industrial linkage that most universities find bothersome is that of risk and liability. To protect themselves they typically seek to limit the financial risks by channelling the activities through a limited liability company and/or they take out insurance policies against professional indemnity, supplemented by injunctions to all staff that they must work through the official mechanisms for the university and themselves to get the benefits of such protection.

7.43 Full protection is in practice not so easily achieved, however. As observed, a significant proportion of academics may well choose to operate outside the formal system. Also, the overall question is a complex one, involving two principal, conflicting considerations:

   (a) even if an academic does not register his outside work a university cannot automatically assume that it is protected from the legal consequences of any negligence on his part. It is possible for the client to argue that the academic has been retained precisely because of his well-recognised status as a university employee – an impression that would be encouraged if for instance the academic had conducted his correspondence on university notepaper – and hence that the university as employer could be legally liable;

   (b) on the other hand, there have been cases of professional negligence in which the individual expert providing the advice has been held to be liable, irrespective of the corporate framework within which he was operating. Thus, an individual in a professional firm constituted as a limited liability company may now be sued rather than the company, on the basis that it is his advice, based on his personal professional standing and not on that of the company's, that has been drawn on.

7.44 Irrespective of these complexities, however, it is worth observing that there has, to our knowledge, been only one law suit – and that in the 1930s – brought against a British university on account of the alleged professional negligence of a staff member.

7.45 The Cambridge approach – placing the onus on the individual to protect himself, and denying the responsibility of the University – does not escape these issues entirely. As observed before it has not been put to the test yet. But it has the merit of being simple and comprehensible.

7.46 A further topic that causes concern is the ownership of intellectual property. This is of particular interest at present because of the impending withdrawal from the British Technology Group of the right of first refusal on the commercial rights to know-how generated by research council funded projects. This is a tricky and controversial matter, and there can never be total clarity as to whether an academic's know-how has been accumulated on or off the job and what university resources have been consumed in the process. Nevertheless, it is noteworthy that in a recent report of a specially constituted committee on patents set up by Oxford University, the conclusion was reached that in the case of a typical university research project the rights should be deemed to vest in the employee and not the employer as is more commonly supposed.

7.47 Again the Cambridge approach is simple and it gives a clear incentive to the individual to exploit commercially his know-how himself. A number of universities similarly automatically assign the rights to the individual, though in a rather less explicit manner; this is perhaps not too surprising since there is a long and undisputed tradition that academics who exploit their know-how by publishing books or appearing on radio or television receive all the revenues directly themselves. But probably the majority take as their starting position the ownership to be theirs, and it is essentially in their discretion to allow the academic concerned or any other party to acquire a stake. This is seldom likely to motivate the academic to push vigorously to commercialise his know-how.

7.48 A revealing indication of the benefits of the Cambridge approach can be inferred from the following figures. Of about 2 500 inventions assigned since 1949 to the National Research Development Corporation from all universities, approximately 300 have become revenue earning. In the same period 39 successfully trading high technology business ventures have been set up by Cambridge University members in the Cambridge area; and one could argue that in effect the burgeoning phenomenon, as evidenced by the family tree, derives indirectly from the 'culture' and the opportunities created by the University's open approach.

7.49 In sum, the net effect of the Cambridge approach can be described as "lowering the threshold to commercialisation" of academic know-how, to quote a key phrase from Bullock's study of university-industry matters in the USA (5). Cambridge's policies, as a central element in the University's long-term thinking, have resulted in an atmosphere in the University where commercialisation of know-how is overt, and is well understood and accepted even by those who are not themselves actively involved. The atmosphere is also such as increasingly to encourage individual academics, who want to commercialise their know-how but recognise that they need help to do so, to turn to the University authorities for assistance. This is especially evident in the bioscience fields where, unlike in engineering, the academics have typically had no previous experience of industry. The general consequence is that, with a flourishing activity already established, the authorities may find it easier, if they wish, to play a fuller role themselves, and to do so without fear of suppressing new activity; this would be strictly in response to demand and on a commercial basis.

7.50 These are tricky issues. The Cambridge model cannot be uncritically applied elsewhere, for all the reasons given earlier. In addition, all sorts of contentious matters are bound to arise in operation of a liberal policy, such as definition of the circumstances in which a university staff member is representing the institution or acting in a personal capacity. Universities must be prepared to deal with, say, any abuses of trust implied by a liberal regime, not by creating inflexible roles but rather by being prepared to exercise their discretion wherever necessary. They cannot expect an open policy to result in no problems at all. But there is probably no line a university could pursue on industrial links that does not entail serious risks and potential problems.

7.51 We would stress what we said at the outset of this chapter: there is no single way of doing things, and every institution must proceed in a way that it knows is right for itself and with which it feels comfortable. Nevertheless, the Cambridge experience gives food for thought and these general observations are made in that spirit.

BENEFITS TO THE UNIVERSITIES

7.52 What, it might be asked, is the benefit to a university of the growth locally of high technology industry? Will universities really gain from lowering the threshold of commercialising their know-how, or will it distort their true purpose and character as is sometimes argued?

7.53 One can dismiss at once, in the case of Cambridge, the last question: the University is so diverse and robust that it can withstand such pressure or mould it in a way that is beneficial. There is certainly no evidence but that the University has gained from the phenomenon.

7.54 Some of the benefits are to do with outside perceptions and the image of the University. The phenomenon has reinforced Cambridge's international status as a centre of scientific excellence, and extended it to embrace an impressive range of technological industries. Cambridge is among the forefront of universities in Britain showing government and industry what higher educational and research institutions really can contribute to the national economy, and offering the prospect of being able successfully to move onto the centre stage in future economic growth as is already happening in the United States. At a different but no less important level, the perception of the University by the local community has been enhanced – even if still regarded as boffins, the scientists are seen to be involved in practical business affairs, making money and creating jobs.

7.55 Other benefits are more tangible. The University's computer laboratory has recently received an above-average share of 'new blood' information technology posts in recognition of its outstanding links with industry, and an assistant lectureship in the same laboratory is supported by a group of local high technology companies. The academics themselves maintain that the quality and relevance of their research and teaching are enhanced by involvement in real industrial problems, all the more so in some fields where industrial research is probably even ahead of university work. Students can see at close hand what new technology industry comprises, both by visits and by vacation jobs (which are valuable trial periods for prospective employer and employee alike).

7.56 Similarly, it is easy for local high technology companies to fund research in the University or to collaborate in joint projects. Also, though there have so far been few financial endowments of any scale made by successful academic entrepreneurs, it is not hard to envisage that they will become more frequent and significant. And finally, as noted earlier, the University itself is now making money directly from license agreements with outsiders for exploitation of particular inventions.

7.57 Qualitative and long-term as some of these benefits are, they are real. Together they add up to the enhancement of Cambridge as an intellectually lively university town and a technologically lively business centre.

THE ROLE OF A SCIENCE PARK

7.58 Chapter 5 assessed the role of the science park in the growth of high technology industry in Cambridge. We observed that, after a slow start and while it is still and will always remain only a small part of the total picture locally, it has come over the past few years to play a substantial role and one that is of special significance in helping the phenomenon develop into its next stages. This role is in terms of the distinctive property that it offers on the local market, the focal point that it offers for (some) academic-industry and inter-company contact, and as the symbol it provides to the outside and inside worlds of the development of science-based industry in Cambridge.

7.59 In short, after a little over a decade the science park has begun to fulfil what had always been hoped, even if somewhat vaguely, of it. That this process has taken a considerable period is one of the general lessons of the science park.

7.60 It takes time for a novel scheme to feel its way in the market and to project the right image and offer the right facilities for the markets aimed at. It takes time to cultivate an environment in which fruitful exchanges across different boundaries are readily possible. It takes time for external confidence in the scheme to be built up and for it to be seen as a desirable location by a diversity of organisations.

7.61 Outside Cambridge there are in the UK now nearly 30 science parks linked to higher educational institutions, of which roughly half are available for occupation. Very nearly all the latter are less than two years old, and all of the schemes are much smaller than Cambridge. Despite these differences, there is nothing so far in these developments to suggest that the lesson of how long things take will not apply.

7.62 A further interesting lesson is to do with the location of a scheme in relation to the university. The experience from Cambridge and elsewhere is that physical contiguity is neither a necessary nor a sufficient condition to achieve the desired industry-academic interchange. The Cambridge park is some three miles from the city centre and the relevant University departments, but this has not prevented interaction. Equally there are examples of science parks on university campuses that are pretty moribund affairs. The critical concepts are less to do with physical distance per se, and rather more with time and convenience of access as well as a perception on both sides of mutual interest and benefit.

7.63 A third lesson concerns the mechanisms for marketing and managing a science park in order to achieve its wider technology transfer and development objectives. Cambridge demonstrates the benefits of continuity of structure and of personnel, and in particular of having the mechanism firmly based in the academic community and readily able to operate the internal scientific networks relevant to the problem at hand.

7.64 In Cambridge the arrangements are highly informal; in some other schemes they are highly structured. Looking across all the schemes as a whole, the essential ingredients of successful arrangements appear to be:

(a) those that fit well with the associated academic and other bodies;

(b) high calibre people implementing the arrangements, having the recognised institutional status to do so and the requisite resources at their command;

(c) express policy commitments by the concerned institutions to a scheme's success and to supporting it in all possible ways.

7.65 A fourth lesson revolves around the balance between the public and private sectors in investing in a science park. Financing of the Cambridge park has been exclusively by the private sector. Initially this was because, given its special historical and financial circumstances and also the more or less zero opportunity cost of the land, Trinity College was able to take a long view of the development. But its willingness to invest in the second and subsequent phases has been very much a function of the strength of demand that it could confidently foresee.

7.66 There are now under way in Britain several university-linked developments that are financed wholly, or very nearly so, and in some cases also managed by the private sector; they are all in economically buoyant areas which are also favoured locations for high technology industry. Equally, there are other such schemes, less advantageously located, which began and have remained more or less exclusively in the control of the public sector. In some of the latter cases the absence of the private sector has not been for want of their being wooed by the public authorities; in others the (mostly modest) participation of the private sector has been induced only by substantial public subsidies or by other, exceptional factors.

7.67 The Cambridge park does not illuminate the particular issue of the tension between the private sector developer/financier and the university – Trinity College happily, and exceptionally, embraces both interests. Experience elsewhere shows that these interests can be reconciled without too much difficulty, provided demand is strong enough.

7.68 Finally, although implicit in what was said earlier it is worth drawing out more fully the role of a science park, as a property development, in promoting high technology industry. The lesson from Cambridge, and indeed from every other situation that we know of, is that provision of property is not itself a sufficient factor. A science park can be helpful in playing particular roles at different stages of development and in helping change attitudes; there are also cases where it can be decisive in enabling a particular project to go ahead. But other ingredients are needed too, and in their absence investment in the property would not be worthwhile.

8

THE FUTURE OF THE PHENOMENON: PROSPECTS AND ISSUES

INTRODUCTION

8.1   There is, as amply evident from earlier chapters, a long history in Cambridge of the University's scientific excellence leading to development of particular sectors of local industry. Nevertheless, in its present form and scale as well as pace of change the Cambridge phenomenon must be understood as still essentially very young. How it will 'mature' and grow, what influences will bear critically on this development, and what the implications will be of continuing development, are matters of great interest from many different points of view. They are national not just local issues, given the scale and significance of the phenomenon.

8.2   This chapter sets out to explore these issues. To help understand the purpose of the chapter, it is important to appreciate what it is not. It is not about predictions, quantitative or otherwise; it is not to do with setting different possible scenarios for the future; and nor does it seek to make any recommendations, though there are policy implications in some of the observations and conclusions. It has been beyond our brief to treat these topics, important as they are, in the depth they necessarily require.

8.3   This chapter is thus put forward in order to help identify, and encourage discussion about, some of the key issues that arise that will shape the future evolution of the phenomenon, whether as a cause or as a consequence of it. Its coverage is necessarily selective; and it should also be noted that the purely business aspects of the issue, as apply at the level of the individual company, are not discussed beyond what was said in chapter 6.

DEVELOPMENT OF THE CORPORATE SECTOR

8.4   We should state at the outset that we are optimistic about the long-term prospects for high technology industry in the Cambridge area. Of course there are many imponderables and many unpredictable external factors that could damage these prospects – for instance if public confidence in the USM (unlisted securities market) were to wane – but such uncertainties cannot sensibly be more than noted in a discussion of this kind.

8.5   Our confidence is based on ten main sets of factors. First, even though the phenomenon is concentrated in a few sectors there is still a good deal of diversity in terms of the particular products and markets and of the firms involved. Rather as applies in the case of the structure of the local economy as a whole, the high technology sector is not so specialised in a very few products or so dominated by a few major companies that it is excessively vulnerable to outside changes or untoward decisions. In these respects Cambridge is somewhat akin to the highly diverse technological base in the Boston area, rather than to Silicon Valley in California where semiconductors were originally the dominant high technology industry and it has been only in the past 10–15 years that significant diversification has taken place.

8.6   Second, there is no reason to doubt the ability of the University and associated research bodies to maintain their record of scientific excellence and to continue to make significant advances which have industrial application. The departments and disciplines that have so far played such a vital role continue to work at the leading edges of their various disciplines; the work of other powerful departments is in areas such as the neurosciences, image processing and materials sciences in which opportunities for commercial exploitation are increasing (1); and new research groups have been created, such as in biotechnology, to constitute a focal point for the University's work in promising fields.

8.7   Public expenditure restraints are already having an impact on Cambridge, as elsewhere, both in the University and in units funded directly by the various research councils; such pressures will no doubt continue. This is a problem that faces British science generally and not just that in Cambridge. The chances must be good, however, that the quality of work in Cambridge will afford a relatively high degree of protection from severe cuts, both directly and also indirectly through the ability to generate alternative sources of funds from the private sector.

8.8   There are also a number of well established and large research programmes, in which the University and major public and private sector technological organisations are collaborating; a project based on the science park and involving the engineering department, British Telecom and General Electric is a good example. Moreover, in the biosciences sphere in particular there is now a substantial degree of interest being shown by commercial firms (mostly foreign-owned) in support for and exploitation of the research activity, which should help cushion the impact of a fall in public sector support.

8.9 One consequence of the restrictions on public expenditure on research is that some individual researchers no longer see their careers as remaining always in the public sector. With the growing number of medical, pharmaceutical and other biotechnological companies establishing in the Cambridge area, there is a corresponding increase in the job opportunities prospectively available to researchers in the various Medical Research Council and other publicly funded institutes: already there is evidence of people from the latter being attracted to the former by much higher salaries and possibly greater research opportunities.

8.10 Taking all these points together, there are good grounds for believing that there will continue to be a high level of advanced research activity in Cambridge and associated with it a flow both of technology showing industrial potential and of people interested to develop the potential. Perhaps the mix and organisation of research will change, with the private sector playing a larger role than before, but if anything that reinforces the point.

8.11 Third, the position and outlook among the long-established companies is generally favourable. In some of them, Cambridge Instruments for instance, major restructuring exercises have recently been gone through and there is a return to sound growth and profitability. In another case, the international conglomerate Dalgety has decided to concentrate its group research activity, especially in advanced agricultural and biotechnological fields, in its existing research and technology centre in Cambridge. This latter development is very much a reflection of the company's confidence in Cambridge as a location for high technology industry in general and biotechnology in particular.

8.12 Fourth, the sheer number of young companies is now such that the probability of at least a few of them growing to be large international businesses is greatly increased; several of them are already heading this way, though one must recognise that it is early days yet and the international markets they operate in are fiercely competitive and becoming more so. The benefits to Cambridge of this happening will be considerable: further enhancement of prestige, an enlarged subcontract sector and perhaps in due course benefactions to the University.

8.13 Fifth, the processes of spinning-out of new firms from existing firms will continue. The family tree given in chapter 3 highlighted this as the major source of new company formation. Again as a consequence of the large absolute number of firms now present, this importance cannot but continue. Further, to go on the American experience: even if some of the small firms get acquired by larger firms, it is quite likely that the individualism of the founders of the former will reassert itself after a period and they will spin out again and this time with greatly increased business experience. More generally, as such experience in the local economy as a whole continues to build up, so one can expect the management and commercial sophistication of all new spin-outs from whatever source steadily to improve. The 'recycling' of people, which has already started happening, will as it continues contribute materially to the maturing and expansion of the phenomenon.

8.14 Sixth, as evident from the discussion of previous chapters a distinctive feature of the Cambridge phenomenon is the commitment to the area felt by the leading personalities and the business community in general. One expression of this is found in, for instance, the support for and continuing involvement of several of the most successful high technology businessmen in the Cambridge ITeC (information technology centre, which offers training in a range of computer skills to unemployed youngsters) – as a result of which it is regarded as one of the most advanced ITeCs in the country.

8.15 Another expression of this commitment and confidence in the area, more directly material to the future of the phenomenon, is investment by successful local companies and individual entrepreneurs, now with considerable personal wealth, in new local ventures perhaps in different technologies and market sectors. There is now a rising incidence of such cases: a well-known example is the financial and other support provided by Acorn Computers to IQ Bio, a 1981 spin-out from the University's biochemistry department.

8.16 Seventh, the increasing availability and sophistication of financial and business services will continue to strengthen the young company sector, by helping both to overcome problems and to take new market opportunities. The informal (even if tough) style of some of the London-based venture capital firms and other financing bodies becoming active in Cambridge, and the qualities brought to bear by highly experienced individuals or small groups of businessmen now operating on the Cambridge 'network', are particularly well suited to playing this role. The international accountancy and management consultancy practices that have set up in Cambridge over the past few years similarly add to the local business scene by contribution to extension of the network of contacts and opportunities especially for the somewhat older and better established high technology firms.

8.17 Eighth, in effect a combination of several of the previous points, a number of new-style venture management firms are setting up in Cambridge: small, technologically very strong and possibly specialised, seeking to play a hands-on management role in the companies they support, and locally founded by people recycling from other high technology companies in the area. These companies have come into existence specifically to offer practical management support to existing companies, which may be in trouble or that cannot cope on their own with growth, and to start-up ventures, in both cases backed up by venture finance as appropriate.

8.18 Ninth, in the same way as outside business financial interests have become active in Cambridge so has the property development industry been attracted. An unprecedented number of new, high technology or similar property schemes are committed or being planned; although they raise many difficult and controversial problems (discussed further in the next section), their effect is also to provide the companies with an appropriate range of choice of property and to ensure that growth of the phenomenon is not constrained by lack of sufficient and suitable accommodation.

8.19 Tenth, and last, a growing number of international high technology companies have become interested in setting up in Cambridge; this again reflects the growing awareness in industrial circles (so far foreign rather more than national) of what is developing in Cambridge. This trend is interesting and very important in its own right. What makes it of special, additional interest is that in several cases the companies' interest has been deliberately cultivated by researchers and particular departments and specialist units in the University. The researchers already had connections with the companies but saw the benefits that would accrue all round if the latter were to set up sizeable operations locally.

8.20 Among the major companies that actually have set up in the past few years are Schlumberger (French-American group engaged in all aspects of drilling technology) which was already collaborating with applied mathematicians and mineralogists in the University; Napp Laboratories and various pharmaceuticals and biotechnology companies of the Dutch AKZO group; the US pharmaceuticals firm Warner Lambert (which had links with the University pathology department); IBM, which has established a 'listening post' on the science park; and Logica, the UK's largest independent software and systems house.

8.21 The case of Logica is instructive. It has recently established its UK technical centre in Cambridge as the focal point of the company's wide-ranging international work in intelligent knowledge-based systems and very large-scale integration initially, and in other emerging technologies especially software engineering. Logica chose Cambridge because of its already close links with the University and other high technology companies in the area, its belief that Cambridge offers the best UK location for recruiting people with the leading-edge skills required, the international prestige of the address, and the proximity to London where Logica's headquarters and main operations are based.

8.22 The arrival in some numbers of international companies such as these – and we know of others who are seriously considering doing so, both as sizeable research groups and as listening posts – marks in general terms the emergence of the phenomenon into a new phase of development which reinforces what has gone before. It introduces new skills, especially in corporate management, and a new, more internationally aware and sophisticated style to the area. It should also induce, by virtue of above-average salary levels, appreciable local multiplier effects through purchasing of personal services; and in the longer term there should be similar benefits through sub-contracting. And – along with the venture management and consultancy firms mentioned earlier – it starts to establish in the locality companies that, because they have substantial resources and a first-hand feel for the Cambridge 'style', will be well placed to play a constructive role in strengthening of the very small highly specialised firms sector that is likely to be needed in the future (see chapter 6).

8.23 This last point is worth developing. For the several reasons discussed earlier – difficulties in sustaining a continued programme of research/design/development and of new product introduction, and in developing international marketing strength, and the like – a proportion of the young companies cannot be expected to survive in their present, highly specialised and independent form. Remarkably little of this has occurred in Cambridge so far (see chapter 3), but the American experience suggests its likelihood. For instance the study referred to previously of 250 high technology firms founded on the San Francisco peninsula during the 1960s showed that by 1980 only 31% were still surviving and independent, 32% had been acquired by other larger firms and 37% had ceased trading (4).

8.24 The possible emergence of this trend does not mean that the start-up and very small firms sector in Cambridge will necessarily decline absolutely. Rather we think just the opposite is likely: as increasing numbers of niche markets emerge and as more people have small business experience, so the sector is likely to thrive and grow. But the processes of growth of the individual firm, once established, are likely to call for greater resources than all of them can mobilise individually, and so some consolidation and rationalisation will be inevitable.

8.25 The question in this context is: how will such strengthening of the sector be effected? A major role will clearly be played by the specialist venture management, consultancy and other business services firms now established in the area, some of them with objectives aimed precisely at this market.

8.26 Another possible, complementary way in which rationalisation and consolidation will be achieved is via acquisition by larger firms. An important question here is: which are the likely acquiring firms? In addition to the categories discussed above of larger international companies with a Cambridge presence, a possible group is indigenous Cambridge companies that are proving successful; in fact some acquisitions have already been made by both these categories. Beyond this, while most financial institutions appear loath to take the initiative in bringing about mergers and take-overs, we are aware of several international venture capital firms who are looking out for investing in medium-sized high technology firms that appear well suited to taking over very small such firms; their searching and acquiring role is of course a national or even international task and by no means confined to Cambridge alone. It may be noted in passing that in general the very large advanced technology UK companies have not been particularly active on the Cambridge scene, and in any event their management style does not usually match well that of the typically rather informal Cambridge firm.

8.27 A further obvious category of likely acquiring firms is foreign companies, and USA companies in particular. This is invariably a controversial topic, and it is important to try and understand the various issues involved.

8.28 Experience in Cambridge is so far limited, but at the level of the individual enterprise that has been acquired there seems little doubt but that acquisition by a much larger US company has been beneficial. The latter has been able to provide an integrated combination of management, international marketing and financial resources than the young acquired company could not mobilise in the UK or hope to generate internally in the short time that the highly competitive markets demanded. (Without in any way decrying, in fact just the opposite, the evidently greater facility of US companies in this respect, it must be a matter of concern in the UK that major national companies have so far apparently been unable to play this role.)

8.29 At a sectoral level the issue is rather less clear-cut, and is conveniently illustrated by the case of computer aided engineering design. It is widely agreed that in the 1970s the UK (in effect, Cambridge – see earlier chapters) had a world lead across a wide range of this technology, and that the USA was similarly well ahead in the design and production of the hardware needed to run the CAD software. Each side clearly needed the other; in the case of the UK the need for a US connection was underlined by the fact that the US constituted by far the largest market for CAD (perhaps 50% of the world market as against 5% for the UK). The question must be asked from a UK national point of view whether there might not have been in aggregate too sizeable a transfer to the USA of CAD know-how and an associated loss of control over its future commercial exploitation. In effect, from this wider standpoint could different deals have been done which would have been strategically better for the UK?

8.30 There is clearly not a simple answer to this question and we do not attempt to take this particular aspect of the matter further. The real reason for raising it is not because of the essentially historic interest in the case of CAD, but rather because the general topic of foreign takeovers and the structuring of deals involving acquisition of know-how by foreign interests continues to be highly relevant in Cambridge. The current attention being paid especially (but by no means exclusively) by American companies to Cambridge research know-how – notably in the medical and biosciences and in the materials sciences, to name but a few fields outside the engineering and computing sectors – is on the one hand very reassuring and is also potentially an excellent way of encouraging foreign interest and one hopes ultimately foreign investment in Britain. On the other hand, there arises the question of whether the strong bargaining position of the scientist will be fully reflected in the outcome of what negotiations may take place and whether the country's strategic economic interests will be best served by the aggregate outcome of the individual negotiations.

8.31 A question of a rather different kind is what form the phenomenon will take – will Cambridge continue to be concentrated on research, design and development with only limited, mostly specialised, production activities or will there be a trend to a higher incidence of production, perhaps even in some volume? There certainly will be individual companies, perhaps many, getting increasingly involved in production of hardware, as they 'harden' in accordance with the model of company development outlined previously.

8.32 We think that in general terms the answer is fairly straightforward. Cambridge's comparative advantage does not lie in volume production: there is no history of this in the area; the national shortage of production management and engineering skills is probably more evident in Cambridge than in most industrial locations; and the existing sub-contract sector is small and specialised, and comprises small companies geared up and cost-efficient only for very short production runs. These considerations are reinforced by the way the relevant industries are organised: there is now a well-established pattern (emphasised in Cambridge but applicable world-wide) of sub-contracting large-scale sub- and final-assembly work to plants specially set up for this purpose and that could be located anywhere. At present Cambridge firms place bulk sub-contract work with companies in various parts of the UK and increasingly overseas notably in South East Asia.

8.33 Nevertheless, it is inevitable – and probably necessary to the future health of the phenomenon – that there will be an increase in hardware production directly in the Cambridge area. Development of high technology industry in the USA has followed this pattern; greatly facilitated in the case of the Route 128 phenomenon around Boston by the presence of highly developed production and management skills due to the long history of industrialisation in the area (12, 14). We do not see Cambridge emulating this on any large scale, for the reasons given earlier, but as individual research, design and development companies grow and new ones get established there will be significant new business opportunities to meet the required increase in the aggregate capacity for 'few-off' specials production and limited production of standard goods. The existing sub-contract sector could not cope with much growth in demand; in any event production runs of any length, though still trivially short by international standards, typically have already to be sub-contracted out of the area. Hence, as the phenomenon evolves, opportunities for local expansion of manufacturing will continue to arise and will need to be taken. The implications of this discussion are considered in the next section.

8.34 Finally, to sum up our most important conclusion: we see no danger of the 'bubble bursting'. We think the phenomenon is now well and truly established and although there will inevitably be business failures and other reversals it is robust enough to withstand them and to continue to grow.

IMPLICATIONS FOR PHYSICAL DEVELOPMENT
8.35 If the business prospects of the phenomenon are favourable, as suggested above, it is clearly important to consider what their implications are for other important 'variables' on the Cambridge scene or, to put it differently, what factors might prevent these prospects from being realised. In Cambridge, given the long history of debate about the size and development of the city, it is quite easy to identify the key issues if there is to be growth – how much? what kind? where?

8.36 This section discusses these questions without, for the reasons given at the start of the chapter, trying to answer them directly and certainly not quantitatively. We are only too aware of the local sensitivities involved, and it was beyond our brief to examine the many detailed issues that would have been necessary to permit full and balanced answers.

8.37 It should be recognised at the outset that growth of high technology industry is by no means the only source of pressure on the physical capacity of Cambridge. The city continues to thrive as a market centre, for shopping and recreation and other purposes. It is positively booming as a tourist attraction – in the 1983 season there were over 3 million visitors (about 55% foreign) who spent around £110 million locally. And the English language schools currently have an annual throughput of approximately 14 000 students (greater than the University's total student numbers).

8.38 To return to the central theme and to start with the question of the size of Cambridge. There are two vital, conflicting considerations. One is that Cambridge is still at that early stage of development as a high technology business centre where it needs to grow. If it does not, it will not achieve a sufficient scale, choice and flexibility in the availability of highly skilled labour and specialised services that will ensure that it remains an attractive location for both employer and employee.

8.39 The microcomputer design and CAD software sectors in Cambridge help illustrate the point. There is now a sufficient pool of highly skilled labour to allow employers to feel confident they can get the people they need. Equally, highly skilled people, including those recruited from elsewhere to the area, feel reassured that there are other firms that could employ them and hence that they have a real choice of jobs beyond their immediate one.

8.40 If the phenomenon is to be sustained and is to mature, the situation in these two sectors must come to apply more widely. At the technological level an obvious category where a larger labour pool will be needed is biotechnology; and at the industrial level, the local capability for engineering production will need to be enlarged. More generally middle to senior managers, with financial, marketing and production skills, and technicians in a variety of fields (laboratory analysis, precision instruments, PCB design and so on) will also be needed. Only very few metropolitan labour markets with large travel-to-work areas can expect ever to have a sufficient diversity and depth of supply to meet every skill needed. Clearly Cambridge – by virtue

of its past employment structure, scale and location – is nowhere near this situation.

8.41 The second consideration, that is in conflict with the case for expansion, arises from concern for the impact of such growth on the nature of Cambridge. The history and the strength of this view, discussed in chapter 2, need not be repeated. But it must be noted that growth has continued apace. The immediate pressure of growth is felt not so much in the city itself – the population in 1983 was 101 000, only some 2% above that 12 years before – but more acutely in the surrounding general catchment area. For instance, the resident population in that part of the travel-to-work area outside the city boundaries reached 83 000 in 1983, approaching the size of the city and representing an increase of 24% compared with 12 years before.

8.42 Furthermore, it is worth emphasising that in this context the conservative attitude to growth is based on much more than sentiment – rather it is central to how successfully Cambridge functions as a university, as a city and as a high technology business centre. If Cambridge were to get so large that the peculiar intimacy and efficiency of its social and business networks were to break down, or that there were to be insufficient interchange between the different sets of networks, or that many people would avoid the city centre because of traffic and parking problems, then that too would be quite counter-productive to the area's economic prosperity.

8.43 So the issue is really how to manage growth, rather than whether or not there should be growth at all. To illuminate this question from the particular vantage point of this study, it is useful to consider the likely pattern of locational demand by high technology companies in relation to what is actually happening in the business property market now.

8.44 In Cambridge and its immediate environment, five distinct kinds of property development are currently taking place or are planned:
    (a) provision of nursery units of modest quality, and similarly of managed workshop space along with some shared services. Such provision, which has so far been on a small scale and is variously located in industrial and commercial areas, has catered principally for 'ordinary' light industrial and other firms, but they have been attractive to some high technology firms at

the start-up stage;

(b) provision of good quality office-style premises on gap or redevelopment sites in established business areas. Those schemes that have recently been completed have proved attractive to small high technology firms that were already established and are expanding, moving up-market and/or are consolidating their premises in a single location, and to firms moving to Cambridge from outside;

(c) development of land on the periphery of the central area, to create high quality, landscaped technology parks and incubator buildings offering a range of property for advanced technology purposes and with supporting services available of various kinds. One such scheme is currently under construction on land on long lease from the county council and next to its own offices only some 10 minutes walk away from the city centre. At least one other broadly equivalent scheme is under construction and another is being planned, though both marginally more distant from the centre. These schemes are likely to cater for the same categories of demand as noted in (b) above, along with new starts, but on a much larger scale;

(d) development of sites on the periphery of the town, aiming for the demand categories in (c) above plus sizeable prestigious projects requiring a great deal of space. Further development of the Trinity College science park is a clear example of this kind of scheme, as is the development proposed by St John's College as well as that proposed on farm land in the green belt just on the city side of the A45 by-pass south of Histon;

(e) 'one-off' developments of sizeable individual properties by longer-established successful local firms. These have so far been on the outskirts of Cambridge or a little further away: they have been undertaken on a freehold and custom-designed basis, usually involving a combination of refurbishment (in some cases of fine old halls or mill buildings) and new-build.

8.45 There are five notable features of all this development activity. First, with the exception of the small workshop units for which the city council is responsible, all are being undertaken or proposed by the private sector. Second, in the new developments, there is a distinct improvement in the quality of property relative to what has been generally available up to now. Indeed some of the new buildings are truly outstanding in architectural terms. Third, as confidence builds up in the property industry and perhaps also as the nature of the Cambridge market is better understood, so there is

evident a greater willingness to let property on shorter and more flexible terms. Fourth, associated with this, provision is concentrated on the high technology sector and there is relatively little property being developed for 'ordinary' industry. Fifth, there is a clear trend to extension of the central business area and to development of new business areas on the outskirts of the city.

8.46 As a consequence of these trends, based on our consultations with the firms and others, we can foresee a situation in which (very roughly):

(a) new and very young small high technology firms without specialised property needs will tend to concentrate in the centre;

(b) somewhat larger but still small firms, demanding and being able to afford quality property, will be concentrated outside the centre (those that actually move out of the centre will create space for the small firms). Those that are not too large and want to be within very easy access of the centre will be concentrated on the schemes noted in paragraph 8.44(b). And those to which these considerations do not apply will go to schemes such as the science park or further away to places like Bar Hill, Huntingdon, St Ives, Melbourn and Sawston which have good connections with Cambridge; and perhaps also to Royston and Saffron Walden, which are closer not only to London but also to Harlow and Letchworth where there are sizeable electronics industries;

(c) much larger and prestigious firms or projects will, as has happened up to now, locate on say the science park or look a little further afield for individual development opportunities.

8.47 This is quite obviously a crude and unquantified model of the property market, and there will not be as rigid a delineation between the different segments of demand as implied. Nevertheless, it fits well with how the existing high technology firms see their property needs and with what is happening by way of new development. And certainly it indicates that not only will availability of property continue not to be a constraint on high technology growth in Cambridge but that it will increasingly no longer be the hassle that it has been in some instances in the past.

8.48 A matter of considerable interest to the county planning authorities is the degree to which growth of the phenomenon can be attracted to locations outside Cambridge, partly to reduce the pressure on the city and partly to provide employment opportunities in areas of greater need notably the Fens and Peterborough. The latter location is of special interest, because of its new town status, its abundance of residential and industrial property, its long history of manufacturing and its active policies for marketing itself as an industrial location.

8.49 Our judgment is that at this stage of the phenomenon there should be only very modest expectations that high technology companies will want to locate away from Cambridge itself and those other main employment locations which have close links with Cambridge. This study has highlighted the importance of Cambridge to high technology industry as a place, as a name, as a network of business contacts, and in all its other senses. There are powerful reasons for high technology companies wanting to be part of the Cambridge scene, and if they were prevented from doing so it would undoubtedly have an adverse impact on the phenomenon.

8.50 As the phenomenon continues to grow, however, labour and property market pressures will build up in the primary locations (and the firms that are highly successful and grow very big will need Cambridge less and have a wide variety of locational choice). One consequence is that more distant locations could be expected to be drawn into the sphere of influence of the phenomenon. It is not hard to see, for instance, that if growth continues at Huntingdon then a next stage of growth would be at Peterborough. But in general there is not now any sense of affinity between Cambridge and Peterborough as business locations, and we think it is some years before Peterborough will become a 'natural' location for companies in the Cambridge phenomenon.

8.51 Peterborough has a relevance in another particular respect. This is that it is especially well suited as a location for companies undertaking medium to large-scale production, which Cambridge is not. In the light of the discussion in the preceding section Peterborough could thus be a suitable location to accommodate production activities that would enlarge Cambridge's present limited capacity. Peterborough is also one of the best locations in the county for larger-scale mobile industrial projects. It could thus well be that such a project gets established in Peterborough specifically with a view to establishing technological links with

Cambridge; there are a few Peterborough firms that already have such connections.

8.52 Despite Peterborough's obvious attractions, however, we wonder whether there might not be a case for permitting establishment in the Cambridge area of a limited number of medium-sized projects in manufacture of high technology goods. Our reasoning is twofold. First, it would at once enlarge the local production and precision engineering capacity. Second, it would introduce skills into the local labour market, notably in production engineering and management, that will in time be helpful to the young companies as they develop; it is striking how much recruitment into such posts has taken place from the few larger manufacturing companies already in the area. Such projects would of course greatly increase demand for various technical skills that are already in short supply and so there would have to be an associated increase in training provision.

8.53 The picture painted so far in this chapter is one of continued buoyancy and growth: expansion and diversification of the phenomenon, accompanied and facilitated by physical development, in a thriving educational, market and tourist centre. It was argued earlier that further growth of the phenomenon is both necessary and desirable. But it must be asked: is there not a real danger that what is now starting to happen, especially since the national property development industry has become so interested in the area, will become counter-productive in the ways previously discussed?

8.54 There clearly is such a danger. The housing market, both in the city and in the surrounding villages, is under great pressure; and the shortages are probably most evident in precisely those categories likely to appeal to professionals and middle-senior management personnel. Commuter traffic and city centre car parking are also problematic, which will be only marginally eased by the pattern of employment decentralisation that is evolving.

8.55 Two further factors could add to these growth pressures. The first, that could have a profound impact on the future of Cambridge, would be if Stansted were given the go-ahead as the third London airport. At an almost trivial, though beneficial level, it would mean much easier air travel for Cambridge businessmen than is at present possible; though completion of the London orbital motorway system in 1986 will make possible easy and fast access to Heathrow. The real impact would be felt, negatively in pressures on the housing market and in spreading urbanisation, and positively in terms of greatly increasing the size of the labour market effectively serving Cambridge and in enhancing the attractiveness of Cambridge to international companies investing in the UK. It would also concentrate development in the south of the county, and reinforce Cambridge's own orientation in that direction.

8.56 The second is to do with the longer-term multiplier effects of the growing success of Cambridge as a high technology business location. Demand for hotels, restaurants, various other personal services, recreational and other amenities – not to mention housing and schooling – will grow as a function of both more people and higher incomes. The available evidence – based on that of the New England economy (17) – is that these services sectors are likely to become quantitatively more significant in employment and output terms than the primary 'engine' of growth, viz high technology industry.

8.57 Taking these growth pressures and their potential impact in conjunction with the need to ensure the continued central role of Cambridge itself, it is evident that planning and management of the area's physical development will demand unusual foresight, skill and strength. There must be scope for many imaginative initiatives – such as introduction of a radically higher quality and more flexible passenger transport system serving the city – in which the public and private sectors might combine.

8.58 All in all, there are thus major challenges to be met – and opportunities to be taken – in the formulation of physical development policies consonant with the future development of the high technology sector. The phenomenon is of national not just local consequence, and so it is a matter of wide concern that a physical development strategy is pursued that is conducive to realisation of the phenomenon's maximum future potential. Clearly this means that a strategy for growth must be tempered by policies that do not damage the Cambridge style and 'culture' that have been so crucial to fostering the phenomenon thus far.

8.59 An interesting feature of the phenomenon over the past 15 years has been the continuing emergence of new physical planning pressures. By and large these have been extremely well dealt with, and the danger has been avoided of seeking to impose all-embracing and hence simplistic planning rules. At a more general level, the Cambridge experience shows that definitions of what constitutes 'acceptable' uses of land and buildings – whether because of changes in the nature of industry and its environmental impact or because of changes in perceptions of the potential role of particular premises and sites (including even green belt land) – cannot sensibly be fixed rigidly for ever. The exact circumstances in each high technology location will be specific to itself, but we are sure that a general lesson that can validly be drawn from Cambridge is that planning policies must be allowed continuously to evolve in ways that are specific to local conditions.

IMPLICATIONS FOR THE LABOUR MARKET

8.60 In addition to the earlier discussion essentially about the scale of the labour market, there are two particular issues worthy of comment. The first is to do with skill shortages. Relative to the rest of the country there is evidently not a shortage of entrepreneurial and advanced technological skills, though as seen from a Cambridge standpoint there could always be more entrepreneurs and it is never easy to recruit technologists of the right calibre and experience.

8.61 Also, looking ahead as the young companies continue to grow and mature so it can be expected that the chronic national shortage of people with advanced information technology skills will become increasingly keenly felt. Arrival in the area of large companies – both technological and financial and business services – will similarly continue to add further pressure to the labour market.

8.62 The more serious skill shortages that are already evident are at the middle-senior management level especially in the marketing, financial and production fields, and in a variety of skilled engineering and technical fields such as PCB design and assembly. In respect of the former, while the technological entrepreneurs are typically quick to acquire basic business skills and increasing numbers of outside businessmen are being drawn into the Cambridge scene, there nevertheless remains a shortfall in the availability of sophisticated business skills of the kinds noted. There is no quick or easy solution to remedying these deficiencies, especially as many of the businesses are breaking new ground in a variety of respects. In a postscript we make further observations on some wider aspects of management education in relation to small high technology business development.

8.63 In respect of the shortages of skilled manual and technical workers, this is not a topic we explored much beyond noting the problems employers said they had. The concern for the future is that there will be a significant increase in demand for these skills as the existing young companies continue to expand; and that this may not be accompanied by a concomitant increase in supply, especially as the small firms cannot mobilise the resources to provide training themselves. Not enough is known in general about the determinants of supply of particular skills in an individual labour market. Certainly in the case of Cambridge it is not clear what have been the relative roles up to now of the various colleges of further education and of large employers providing formal in-house training, and what will induce increased supply in the future. A so-called local collaborative project, sponsored jointly by the Manpower Services Commission and the Department of Education and Science, is currently under way in Cambridge; this may provide a pointer on these issues. As a general comment, however, we would observe that skill shortages of all the different kinds discussed are likely to become more serious than they have been in the past, and the subject is worthy of proper study and appropriate action.

8.64 The second comment to make about the labour market is of a rather different kind. It is simply to observe that the phenomenon is generating a significant number of job opportunities in the business services field, which women (not necessarily graduates but having good previous business experience) are well suited to fill. It seems that such women find it congenial to work alongside young technologists and professionals who have contemporarily liberal attitudes on the role of women in employment. Interestingly, however, we are aware of only a handful of cases in which women are among the principals in the high technology companies themselves.

CONCLUDING COMMENTS

8.65 To repeat what was said earlier: the Cambridge phenomenon now has firm foundations and substantial potential for sustained future development. Although still quite small in scale, it represents one of the very few spontaneous growth centres in a national economy that has been depressed for all of a decade – and certainly the only one where growth is being led by high technology industry, and indigenous and small companies at that.

8.66 It is thus clearly a phenomenon of national significance. As such it is a matter of widespread interest how it develops, and indeed that it should develop as successfully as possible. The business and physical development issues – separately and also inter-connectedly – discussed in this chapter must be addressed with much skill and imagination, bearing in mind that the phenomenon has "grown like Topsy" and that the natural effervescence of the area must not be inhibited in the interests of an orderly, managed approach. That the issues are tackled effectively and in the right spirit is of consequence not just in Cambridge alone, but also in many other locations and among public and private sector bodies throughout Britain and indeed elsewhere in Europe and beyond.

9.1   In the course of this study we were struck by the need systematically to develop in the UK more information about and a deeper understanding of the high technology sector and particularly the role of small firms in the sector. The concern arises at two different levels – the individual enterprise, and the public policy context in which the enterprise operates – and at the way they interact.

9.2   At the level of the firm, it is evident from this study that more knowledge is needed of the processes of growth and development of small high technology firms, in order to provide a sound foundation for better management decision-taking and business growth. It is not a theoretical but a practical understanding that is required of the firms' markets and how they evolve and how they can be influenced by technology, of what options they have for entering overseas markets, how they should build up their management teams and organisational structures, and so on. In some respects these issues are the same for any small firm, not just those in high technology.

9.3   But there are marked differences too, essentially because of the combination of high R&D/D&D intensity, short product life cycles, protection of intellectual property, rapid growth prospects and early need for selling to international markets in the case of high technology firms. The combination of these differences is such as to present a whole new set of basic management problems for high technology compared with conventional small firms.

9.4   Strategic and practical business development problems are certainly uppermost in the minds of many of the young companies consulted in the course of this exercise. Probably the most frequently articulated concern is to do with development of management skills and organisational structures, such as to permit international marketing and overall growth without sacrificing the freshness and technological fertility that have made them successful in the first place. There is also a strong interest in learning from the experience of others.

9.5   At the second level there are issues of public policy. Many fields of policy are involved: financial assistance to companies; investment in research and exploitation of the results; foreign investment and technology leakage; mergers and acquisitions; public procurement; university-industry relationships; manpower development; land use and physical planning; and so on. There are complex legal and institutional issues too, which turn on the rights and responsibilities of different parties engaged in commercial exploitation of research carried out in the public sector.

9.6   None of these issues is new per se. It is the need to look at them in an interrelated way and to formulate policies accordingly that is new, and we are not aware that this need is yet being systematically addressed. It is not easy for central government quickly to do so. Inevitably responsibilities are spread among different departments as well as among different groups within the same department. At this stage the whole topic seems to us to lend itself more suitably to academic, though practical, study.

9.7   Up to now Cambridge University has had only a modest provision of business studies courses. The engineering department has, as an option within the engineering degree, successfully run courses in management studies for some 30 years but it is only quite recently that these have been available on any scale. Further advanced courses are soon to be introduced, for which only students who have completed part one of the tripos in engineering, natural science or computing science will be eligible. There is as yet no research in business studies undertaken in the University, though there is a strong record of industrial policy research in the applied economics department. Outside the University, plans are afoot in the private sector to establish a general business school on lines broadly equivalent to the language schools in Cambridge that are proving so successful in attracting foreign students who want to learn English.

9.8   The opportunity we see is for something rather more wide-ranging and with higher research orientation than these existing or planned teaching courses, and at the same time more narrowly focused on the high technology, small company sector itself. A combination of teaching and empirical research must ultimately be aimed at enhancing the management capabilities and improving the performance of these companies. In addition what requires hard practical study is how the small company technological sector interacts with all the dimensions of public policy noted earlier.

9.9   There has from time to time been discussion in Cambridge about the possibility of setting up a business school which would complement the courses already available in the University. Various parties inside and outside the University are currently engaged in discussion about long-term development of business studies in the University, and we hope that the special needs and opportunities presented by the phenomenon will be reflected in whatever practical initiatives may emerge. As a result of the phenomenon and also its leading edge role in so many relevant disciplines, Cambridge is the natural locus for developing a national teaching and research capability in the high technology small business field.

SPONSORSHIP AND ORGANISATION OF THE STUDY

The sponsors of the study were:
Acorn Computer Group PLC
Barclays Bank PLC
Cambridge Consultants Ltd
Cambridge Interactive Systems Ltd
Cambridgeshire County Council
Corpus Christi College, Cambridge
Department of Land Economy, University of
    Cambridge
Emmanuel College, Cambridge
Peterhouse, Cambridge
St John's College, Cambridge
Science & Engineering Research Council
Shape Data Ltd
Sinclair Research Ltd
Topexpress Ltd
Trinity College, Cambridge
UK Department of Trade and Industry
Wolfson College, Cambridge

A steering group was formed to guide the exercise. Its membership was:

Stephen Bragg	*Wolfson Cambridge Industrial Unit*
Vivian Brown/ Philip Gregory	*UK Department of Trade & Industry*
Matthew Bullock (chairman)	*Barclays Bank PLC*
Gordon Cameron	*Department of Land Economy, University of Cambridge*
Geoffrey Cooper	*Science and Engineering Research Council*
Richard Cutting	*Sinclair Research Ltd*
Jack Lang	*Topexpress Ltd*
Peter Whitehead/ Clive Thompson	*Cambridgeshire County Council*

The group met five times at key stages in the exercise, including review of a draft version of this report. It exercised a vital role, since its members variously reflected a body of local and national knowledge and experience that were of enormous benefit to the study team. Nevertheless, in a formal sense the steering group acted in an advisory capacity only and the study team alone remains responsible for the report.

The study was carried out by Segal Quince & Partners. The team comprised Nick Segal, Andrew Gould, Peter Tipple, Charles Monck, Roger Quince and Bill Wicksteed.

Fieldwork on the exercise was carried out between February and June 1984. The draft report was completed in August and was reviewed by the steering group and others in September-November. The final version was completed in December.

Our thanks go first and foremost to:

(a) the sponsors of the study (see appendix A) for their financial and other support;

(b) the study steering group (see also appendix A) who both collectively and individually advised and assisted us in all aspects of the exercise;

(c) the many hundreds of companies, financial institutions, public sector organisations and individuals who gave so generously of their time in our interview programme;

(d) the Department of Trade & Industry, the Scottish Development Agency, the First National Bank of Boston and other organisations that made special efforts to supply us with particular information.

We would like to place on record our special debt of gratitude to Matthew Bullock of Barclays Bank PLC, who not only played the central role in securing sponsorship for the study but also devoted time and effort to its substance that went far beyond the call of duty as chairman of the steering group. Mr Bullock is recognised in Cambridge as having played a unique role in identifying and nurturing the phenomenon when it was still in embryonic form, and in helping speed up creation of the right conditions in which it could flourish.

In addition we would like to thank the following individuals who, although having no formal role in the project, were unfailingly generous in the time and thought they gave to it at various stages:

(a) Dr Ian Nicol (recently retired secretary general of the board of faculties of the University) who, as driving force behind establishment of the Mott committee and author of its report and subsequently as 'strategist' behind the University's policy towards links with industry, has exercised a profound, indirect influence on the phenomenon;

(b) Dr John Bradfield of Trinity College who has played the key role in successful development of all aspects of the Cambridge science park;

(c) Walter Herriot of Barclays Bank PLC in Cambridge, who has been at the forefront of implementing the Bank's strategy for supporting small high technology enterprises;

(d) Dr Bill Nixon of the University engineering department and Peterhouse, Dr Christopher Johnson of St John's College and Christopher Taylor of Corpus Christi College, whose many and various connections with the academic and business communities locally and beyond typify the 'networks' which are so crucial to how Cambridge functions as an academic, social and high technology community.

APPENDIX C
APPROACH AND SCOPE

Introduction

There were two principal elements in our approach to the exercise. One was to build up a computerised data bank on the high technology companies themselves, covering basic facts about their origins, activities, links with other high technology organisations and so on. The other was to consult very widely in Cambridge and outside, to develop an overall picture of the phenomenon and to gain an understanding of its causes. Each of these aspects will now be dealt with separately.

The population of high technology firms

We wanted to construct as complete a list as possible of high technology firms operating in the Cambridge area at the time of our fieldwork. This at once raised two questions: what is a high technology firm and what in this context is the Cambridge area? There were no readily available or a priori answers to these issues; rather we recognised that sensible answers, which along with other factors would lead to a definition of the Cambridge phenomenon, would have to be generated by the study itself. Consequently it will be simpler here to defer consideration of these questions until after we have explained our data sources and field methodology.

One matter is worth highlighting now, however. This is that we started off expressly looking not only at companies in manufacturing but also at those engaged in relevant service sector activities such as contract R&D, scientific consultancy and advanced software development. The nature of technological development especially in the computing and related fields is such that hard distinctions cannot be easily drawn between the services (software) and manufacturing (hardware) sectors. Moreover, especially because it was well known that Cambridge had a high concentration of companies and university-related expertise in precisely these fields, there were sound practical grounds for adopting this wide approach. But it is important to draw attention to it, because so many studies tend to concentrate exclusively on manufacturing industry.

Our starting point for identifying the relevant population of firms was the excellent directory compiled by Cambridgeshire county council. A broad definition was used initially to allow companies to be regarded as potentially eligible for inclusion unless discussions with them revealed them not to be high technology or in any way linked to Cambridge. After extensive consultations we narrowed down our focus to firms throughout the county in the following industrial groups: chemicals, biotechnology and pharmaceuticals; computer hardware and peripherals; electrical and electronic engineering (including telecommunications); instrument engineering; computer software; and R&D (research and development) and scientific and technical consultancy. Where we had the actual knowledge to do so we eliminated from these groups those companies that we judged could not be regarded as properly high technology; for instance, we excluded firms supplying routine computer bureau services.

We then cross-checked this list against the (much smaller) membership of the Cambridge Technology Association, as well as against a comprehensive data bank of manufacturing firms operating in East Anglia in 1981 (11). We also supplemented it from three main sources:

(a) consultations with local authorities outside the county that we felt might potentially have firms that were part of a Cambridge sphere of influence. These included local authorities in Norfolk, Suffolk, Essex, Hertfordshire and Bedfordshire;

(b) advice from other bodies, notably the Council for Small Industries in Rural Areas, with specialist information;

(c) referrals by other companies and word-of-mouth generally as the fieldwork progressed. This continued to be a fruitful though erratic source throughout the exercise, and in the end we had to accept that we could not pursue every lead given to us.

Our final list of companies that prima facie needed to be contacted contained 403 names. We wrote to all the companies explaining the origins and purpose of the study and seeking their cooperation: this was then followed up by a telephone interview and/or face-to-face interview, in both cases using a structured aide-memoire. The companies were assured that the information they provided would be kept confidential to the study team and would be used only in aggregation with that of other companies unless we had their explicit permission to do otherwise.

The 328 telephone interviews, each lasting anything up to 40 minutes, were used to obtain basic data about the origins and activities of the companies, the nature of their products and services, financial and employment aspects, reasons for their choice of location, links of all kinds with the University and other bodies in Cambridge and their own perceptions as to whether or not they were part of the Cambridge high technology scene, and so on. We did not seek to explore their business development problems unless the information was volunteered. Instead we concentrated on getting basic facts about each company and on whether or not it should be counted as part of the Cambridge phenomenon. Again, the interviews were conducted on a confidential basis; in those cases where we have written pen pictures for inclusion in this report a draft version was approved by each firm concerned.

Face-to-face interviews were with companies of two main categories:

(a) small and young companies (some of them already interviewed on the telephone) who were unambiguously part of the phenomenon. The purpose of these interviews was to discuss in depth all aspects of their performance and development, from start-up through critical phases of growth (or otherwise) to their current and prospective position. Thirty-nine such interviews were held, each typically lasting about two hours and occasionally going up to nearly twice that duration;

(b) long-established and large companies, of whom we interviewed 11. Here our aim was to understand their role in the local economy, as employers and otherwise including their links with the University, and to seek to benefit from their perspective on the Cambridge business and high technology scene.

Based on this material we adopted the following 'definitions':

(a) a company would be regarded as 'high technology' for the purposes of compiling our data bank if technological sophistication and/or continuing technological development and innovation were clearly significant characteristics of the business. (We had hoped that a question on R&D expenditure as a percentage of turnover would provide a further important criterion, but we were too doubtful of the quality of the answers to feel confident in using only this measure.) We excluded from the data bank firms providing regular business, professional or financial services to the high technology companies, unless these services were of an advanced nature and themselves involved some R&D. Taking a long view the growth of the business 'infrastructure' in Cambridge is very much part of the phenomenon, as discussed in the report, but we felt it appropriate to include in the data bank primary rather than ancillary producers. Similarly, the data bank excludes those few establishments engaged only in distributive operations; it is possible that some of these might in time introduce production and even R&D activities 'vertically behind' the existing marketing and sales activity and so become unambiguously

part of the phenomenon, but we felt it prudent to leave them out of our statistics at this stage;

(b) a high technology company in the Cambridge sub-region would be regarded as part of the Cambridge phenomenon if, irrespective of its precise location, it had significant technological, market or other links with other organisations in the Cambridge area and if it felt itself actually to participate in the phenomenon.

Adoption of these definitions resulted in the following basic classification of the companies in the overall list we had assembled by end-June 1984:

number of companies on overall list	403
number of companies contacted	362
number of companies not contacted (untraceable etc)	41
number of companies unable or unwilling to be interviewed	34
number of interviewed companies considered not high technology	36
number of interviewed companies having no significant links with Cambridge	31
number of interviewed companies judged to be part of the Cambridge phenomenon	261
estimated number of companies not identified or interviewed but probably eligible for inclusion in the phenomenon	40
estimated total population of high technology companies in Cambridge phenomenon (mid-1984)	c300

We computerised the information on the 261 interviewed companies judged to be part of the phenomenon. We estimate that this sample accounted for around 85% of the mid-1984 population of high technology companies in the Cambridge area. The material was analysed using the University computer laboratory computer.

As noted in appendix A the draft report was completed in August 1984, reviewed in September-November and finalised in December. During the period of review and revision we continued to collect information about the local high technology sector. This principally entailed identification of, and brief interview with, a number of very small companies that had previously slipped through our net (most of them operated part-time by academics) or that had only just started up. In addition a number of outside companies moved into the area. It was too late to incorporate these various businesses in the computerised data bank but they are shown on the family tree chart as appropriate. By end-1984 we had positively identified a total of 322 high technology companies in the phenomenon, and estimated that there were perhaps a further 25 in existence but not identified by us.

Table C.1 gives the sectors used in classifying the company by industry.

TABLE C.1
Description of sectors used in the classification of companies

TITLE	ACTIVITY CODE ACCORDING TO 1980 STANDARD INDUSTRIAL CLASSIFICATION	
Chemicals/ biotechnology	251	Basic industrial chemicals
	256	Specialised chemical products
	257	Pharmaceutical products
Electrical equipment	343	Electrical equipment for industrial use
Electronics capital goods	344	Telecommunications equipment, electrical measuring equipment, electronic capital goods, passive electronic components
Other electronics	345	Other electronic equipment
Instrument engineering	37	Instrument engineering
Computer hardware	3302	Electronic data processing equipment
Computer software	8394	Computer software
Consultancy (R&D)	9400	R&D, scientific and technical consultancy

Finally in this section, unless otherwise stated the money values given in chapter 3 are in terms of mid-1984 prices.

Other fieldwork
The company interviews were augmented by consultations with the following:

(a) senior officers in the University and some of the colleges;

(b) departmental heads and senior researchers in those groups in the University and in the research institutions in the area that were identified as directly relevant to the phenomenon;

(c) local authorities and other relevant public bodies in Cambridgeshire and selectively in adjacent counties;

(d) individuals and organisations based in Cambridge and providing professional and business services to the high technology companies. Those interviewed included accountants, lawyers, patent agents, clearing banks and other financial institutions, property agents, the chamber of commerce and local enterprise agency, and so on;

(e) London-based financial institutions providing specialist services to the high technology companies;

(f) the UK Department of Trade & Industry;

(g) a variety of individuals who by virtue of past or present involvements in Cambridge were able to offer a special perspective on the evolution of the phenomenon.

Altogether we conducted nearly 140 face-to-face interviews in these categories. The format of the consultations was rather more free-ranging than those with the companies, though we again used an aide-memoire to guide the discussion. It was not easy to know where to draw the line in consulting additional people: more or less without exception every new interview generated suggestions as to whom else might be seen. In the end, limitations of time and resources prevented us from consulting all the people we would ideally have liked to.

Caveats
In a study of this nature there are inevitably numerous points of detail which require technical qualification. The more important of these, necessary to understanding of the argument, are picked out in the relevant sections of the report. One general qualification might be noted here, however: for stylistic purposes the words 'firm' and 'company' are used interchangeably even though they strictly are not always the same (the bulk of Cambridge high technology enterprises are in fact limited companies).

The word 'company' (or firm or enterprise) is used loosely in another sense too. It is taken to refer to establishments in the area even where they may not be self-contained enterprises but subsidiary operations of companies based elsewhere (though this latter group is a small proportion of the total). But where there is more than one establishment in the area belonging to the same company, it is counted only once though the relevant information from all the company's local establishments are included in the data bank.

A further qualification is of a different kind. Throughout the text we refer to the companies in the phenomenon as 'Cambridge companies'. This is not strictly accurate since, although the great majority of the firms that can be counted as part of the phenomenon are located in or very close to Cambridge, nevertheless a significant proportion are in towns and villages up to say 15 miles away and a few are even further afield. Correspondingly the focus of the discussion of the geographic spread and the process of the phenomenon is concentrated on Cambridge. This emphasis on Cambridge is not just a stylistic and short-hand convenience: it is central to the phenomenon itself.

1   Advisory Board Research Councils:
'Scientific opportunities and the science budget 1983'
Department of Education and Science 1984

2   Advisory Council for Applied Research and Development with the Advisory Board of Research Councils:
'Improving the research links between higher education and industry'
HMSO June 1983

3   Michael Breheny, Paul Cheshire and Robert Langridge:
'The anatomy of job creation? Industrial change in Britain's M4 Corridor'
Built Environment 9(1) 1983

4   A V Bruno and A C Cooper:
'Patterns of development and acquisitions for Silicon Valley start-ups'
Technovation 1(4) August 1982

5   M P D Bullock:
'Academic enterprise, industrial innovation, and the development of high technology financing in the United States'
Brand Bros London 1983

6   M P D Bullock:
Paper presented to the Fraunhofer Gesellschaft conference:
'Financing of innovations in new and young technology based enterprises', Bonn, October 1984

7   N Carter and C Watts:
'The Cambridge science park'
Surveyors Publications London 1984

8   A C Cooper:
'Spin-offs and technical entrepreneurship'
IEEE Transactions on Engineering Management EM-18(1) 1971

9   Department of Trade & Industry, South East Regional Office:
(a) 'The location, mobility and finance of new high technology companies in the UK electronics industry'
November 1982
(b) 'The location, mobility and financing of the computer services sector in the UK'
March 1983

10   J R Firn and D Roberts:
'High technology industries' in N Hood and S Young (ed):
'Industry, policy and the Scottish economy'
Edinburgh University Press 1984

11   A J Gould and D Keeble:
'New firms and rural industrialisation in East Anglia'
Regional Studies 18(3) 1984

12   J M Howell:
'The role of high technology in the US economy; the New England experience'
The First National Bank of Boston 1984

13   P Jervis:
'Innovation in electron-optical instruments – two British case histories'
Research Policy 1 1971/72

14   Joint Economic Committee (Monetary and Fiscal Policy Sub-Committee) of the US Congress:
'Location of high technology firms and regional economic development – United States'
Paper presented to the OECD Workshop on Research, Technology and Regional Policy, Paris, October 1983

15   D Keeble:
'East Anglia and the East Midlands' in G Manners, D Keeble, B Rodgers and K Warren:
'Regional Development in Britain'
Second edition, Wiley 1980

16   S Lavington:
'A history of Manchester computers'
National Computing Council 1975

17   N S Lee:
'Economic influences governing strategic planning for New England'
The First National Bank of Boston 1984

18   D H McQueen and J T Wallmark:
'Spin-off companies from Chalmers Institute of Technology'
Technovation 1 1982

19   S A Manning:
'Portrait of Cambridgeshire'
Robert Hale 1978

20   B Moore and R Spires:
'The experience of the Cambridge science park'
Paper presented to the OECD Workshop on research, technology and regional policy, Paris, October 1983

21   M J Moseley and M Sant:
'Industrial Development in East Anglia'
GEO Books 1977

22   (The Mott Committee):
'Relationship between the University and science-based industry'
Cambridge University Reporter, 22 October 1969

23   National Governors Association:
'Technology and growth; state initiatives in technological innovation'
US Department of Commerce 1983

24   R P Oakey:
'Research and development cycles, investment cycles and regional growth in British and American small high technology firms'
Centre for Urban and Regional Development Studies, University of Newcastle upon Tyne 1983

25   C W Oatley:
'The early history of the scanning electron microscope'
J Appl Phys 53(2) 1982

26   J Obermayer:
'Case studies examining the role of government R&D contract funding in the early history of high technology companies'
US Department of Commerce 1980

27   L S Peters and H I Fusfeld:
'Current US university/industry research connections'
in National Science Board and National Science Foundation:
'University-industry research relationships – selected studies'
Washington DC 1983

28   E B Roberts and H A Weiner:
'New enterprises on Route 128'
Science Journal December 1968

29   A Saxenian:
'The genesis of Silicon Valley'
Built Environment 9(1) 1983

30   The Washington Post, 3 December 1984
(quoting the Virginia State Department of Economic Development) Washington DC